A Letter to Our Readers
From Bella Robinson, Executive Director of COYOTE RI

Dear Friends,

When I founded **Call Off Your Old Tired Ethics (COYOTE) Rhode Island** in 2009, it was in response to the re-criminalization of prostitution in our state. At the time, I had already spent over 25 years as a criminalized sex worker, and I had experienced firsthand the devastating impact of criminalization. I couldn't report bad actors who tried to harm or exploit me, and I witnessed how threats of eviction, child custody battles, and workplace discrimination were wielded as weapons against sex workers.

These experiences showed me how deeply the stigma of criminalization runs and how it creates an environment where predators and abusers thrive. Over the years, I have seen how the criminalization of sex work has fueled mass incarceration and unjustly contributed to the surveillance of workers. While sex workers have been telling these stories for decades, too often, those in power haven't listened.

The Power of Decriminalization
During the period when indoor prostitution was decriminalized in Rhode Island, I felt a freedom I had never experienced before. Decriminalization allowed sex workers to report violence and exploitation without fear. We could work safely from homes, spas, or agencies, contributing to the economy by paying taxes and operating as legitimate businesses. It was during this time that I saw the transformative potential of decriminalization—and the importance of fighting to preserve it.

Building Knowledge Through Research
One of the greatest challenges in advocating for sex workers' rights
has been the lack of reliable data. In 2017, COYOTE RI
spearheaded a groundbreaking survey of 1,515 U.S. sex workers,
creating the largest dataset of its kind. This project wasn't led by
academics but by a community of criminalized sex workers with a
shared determination to tell our stories.

The survey revealed the lived realities of sex workers and
trafficking survivors, and it became a cornerstone for subsequent
research. In 2018, we launched the "After FOSTA Survey" to
document the immediate impacts of FOSTA/SESTA, and in 2022,
we followed up with the "Four Years of FOSTA" report. These
efforts helped us provide critical data for advocacy, including an
amicus brief challenging FOSTA's constitutionality.

Advocacy Through Education and Coalition Building
I have spent the past decade building coalitions, presenting at
universities, and educating policymakers and the public about the
realities of sex work and criminalization. One of my mentors,
Norma Jean Almodovar, emphasized the importance of presenting
research to students—the future policymakers and voters who will
shape our world.

COYOTE RI's work has also been enriched through partnerships
with organizations like SWOP Behind Bars, the Desiree Alliance,
and the National Council of Incarcerated and Formerly
Incarcerated Women & Girls. These collaborations have
strengthened our advocacy and ensured that sex workers' voices
are included in broader movements for justice and equity.

Lessons Learned and Looking Ahead
In 2024, COYOTE RI published a book based on our survey data
and research. While it wasn't the complete reflection of our
community's efforts that I had hoped for, it served as an important

milestone in documenting our work. The book represents not just data but the resilience, collaboration, and commitment of everyone who contributed to this movement.

As I reflect on the journey of COYOTE RI, I am reminded that the fight for decriminalization is not just for my generation—it is for the next. I may not see full decriminalization in my lifetime, but I am confident that the groundwork we have laid will pave the way for a better future for sex workers.

Thank you for standing with us in this fight. Together, we will continue to amplify the voices of sex workers, challenge unjust systems, and build a world where everyone is treated with dignity and respect.

In solidarity,
Bella Robinson
Executive Director, COYOTE RI

Acknowledgments

This book would not have been possible without the dedication and support of the individuals and organizations that work tirelessly to uplift and advocate for the rights and well-being of sex workers everywhere.

COYOTE Rhode Island is eternally grateful to:

- **The Young Women's Empowerment Project**, who laid the foundations of participatory action research in our community with their groundbreaking reports, *Girls Do What They Have To Do To Survive: Illuminating Methods Used By Girls In The Sex Trade To Heal And Fight Back* and *Bad Encounter Line 2012, A Participatory Research Project: Denied Help! How Youth In The Sex Trade and Street Economy Are Turned Away From Systems Meant to Help Us & What We Are Doing to Fight Back*. These reports, particularly *Bad Encounter Line*, paved the way for the work we do today.
- **The National Council for Incarcerated and Formerly Incarcerated Women and Girls**, for their incredible and inclusive advocacy that has inspired and guided us.
- **Catherine Sevcenko**, Attorney for the National Council for Incarcerated and Formerly Incarcerated Women and Girls, filed our amici brief based on the 2022 *After FOSTA Survey*. Your work was instrumental in amplifying the voices of our community.
- **Selene Means**, who took the stunning cover photo, capturing the spirit of resilience and strength embodied in this work.

To the brave voices who shared their stories and wisdom, thank you for trusting us with your truths. Your courage is the foundation of this work.

To the staff and volunteers at COYOTE Rhode Island, your unwavering commitment to advocacy, harm reduction, and education continues to inspire us all. Your efforts are transforming lives and shaping a more just and compassionate society.

Special thanks to **SWOP Behind Bars**, whose leadership, vision, and relentless dedication have guided this project from inception to completion. Your advocacy for sex worker rights and your commitment to amplifying marginalized voices have made an indelible mark on this work and on the movement as a whole.

To our collaborators, contributors, and supporters—your solidarity and generosity fuel this work. Thank you for believing in the power of community, storytelling, and activism.

Lastly, to the global community of sex workers and allies, this book is for you. May it serve as a beacon of resilience, empowerment, and hope.

With gratitude and solidarity,

Bella Robinson, Executive Director

COYOTE RI

December 17: International Day to End Violence Against Sex Workers

December 17, 2024 marks the 21st Anniversary of **International Day to End Violence Against Sex Workers**, a day of reflection, advocacy, and remembrance for sex workers around the world who have lost their lives to violence or faced systemic injustice. Established in 2003 by Dr. Annie Sprinkle and the Sex Workers Outreach Project (SWOPUSA), this day was created to address the pervasive violence sex workers face and the societal stigma that often leaves these crimes unacknowledged.

The origins of this day trace back to the arrest of Gary Ridgway, the Green River Killer, who confessed to murdering at least 49 women, many of whom were sex workers. Ridgway admitted to targeting sex workers because he believed their disappearances would attract less attention from law enforcement and the public. This tragic revelation exposed deep societal indifference to violence against sex workers and underscored the urgent need for systemic change.

December 17 began as a day to honor Ridgeway's victims and has since evolved into a global movement to highlight the violence faced by sex workers worldwide. It serves not only to mourn those lost but also to advocate for the decriminalization of sex work, legal protections for sex workers, and an end to the stigma that perpetuates their marginalization. Vigils, rallies, and educational events are held globally to honor the resilience of sex workers and challenge the societal attitudes that make them vulnerable. Advocates, activists and allies use the day to amplify the voices of sex workers, demand accountability for crimes against them, and push for policies that prioritize their safety and dignity.

The violence sex workers face is deeply rooted in broader issues of inequality, including racism, sexism, transphobia, and poverty. Marginalized groups within the sex work community, such as transgender individuals, people of color, and migrants, experience intersecting layers of discrimination that heighten their vulnerability. Legal protections are often absent, and societal stigma leaves many sex workers without access to justice, healthcare, or social support.

December 17 reminds us that addressing violence against sex workers requires tackling these systemic issues. It is a call to action for governments, communities, and individuals to challenge harmful stereotypes, support harm reduction strategies, and create a world where sex workers can live and work free from violence and discrimination.

What We've Learned Over 21 Years

1. Systemic Violence Is Rooted in Stigma and Criminalization
The criminalization of sex work exacerbates violence by pushing the industry underground, leaving workers more vulnerable to abuse. Stigma perpetuates this violence, dehumanizing sex workers and discouraging law enforcement, healthcare providers, and policymakers from prioritizing their safety.

2. Intersectionality Amplifies Vulnerability
Marginalized groups within the sex work community are disproportionately targeted by violence due to racism, transphobia, xenophobia, and poverty. Policies addressing these overlapping oppressions must replace the one-size-fits-all approach often applied to sex workers.

3. Access to Justice Is Often Denied
Fear of arrest or further victimization prevents many sex workers

from seeking help from law enforcement. Decriminalization has shown promise in improving access to justice, fostering better relationships with authorities, and reducing violence.

4. Advocacy and Visibility Matter
Sex worker-led organizations and advocacy efforts have brought issues of violence into public discourse, challenging stereotypes and pushing for legislative reforms. Community-led harm reduction strategies, such as safety apps and peer support networks, have proven effective.

What Has Changed

- **Decriminalization and Legal Reforms:** Countries like New Zealand and parts of Australia have decriminalized sex work, leading to reduced violence, improved healthcare access, and better working conditions.
- **Global Awareness:** December 17 and advocacy efforts have increased recognition of sex workers' rights, with human rights organizations now addressing these issues.
- **Technological Advances in Safety:** Tools like bad-date reporting systems, safety apps, and encrypted communication platforms have enhanced information sharing and community solidarity.

What Hasn't Changed

- **Persistent Stigma:** Despite progress, societal stigma against sex workers remains pervasive, fueling discrimination and exclusion from essential services like healthcare and housing.
- **Resistance to Decriminalization:** Many governments continue punitive approaches, such as the "Nordic model," which criminalizes clients and further endangers sex workers.

- **Limited Access to Justice and Resources:** Sex workers still face barriers to reporting violence, with police corruption and indifference persisting as significant obstacles.

Looking Ahead

To end violence against sex workers, efforts must focus on decriminalization, empowerment, education, and intersectional advocacy. Decriminalizing sex work and recognizing it as legitimate labor will protect workers' rights and safety. Supporting sex worker-led organizations ensures policies reflect their lived experiences. Public awareness campaigns can challenge stigma and foster empathy, while addressing the compounded vulnerabilities of marginalized groups will create a more equitable society.

While progress has been made, the fight for justice, safety, and equality for sex workers continues. By learning from the past 21 years and building on the progress achieved, we can work toward a future where sex workers are respected, safe, and free from violence and discrimination.

Dedicated to
sex workers everywhere.

17

Table of Contents

Acknowledgements

This book would not have been possible without the dedication and support of the individuals and organizations that work tirelessly to uplift and advocate for the rights and well-being of sex workers everywhere.

COYOTE Rhode Island is eternally grateful to:

- **The Young Women's Empowerment Project**, who laid the foundations of participatory action research in our community with their groundbreaking reports, *Girls Do What They Have To Do To Survive: Illuminating Methods Used By Girls In The Sex Trade To Heal And Fight Back* and *Bad Encounter Line 2012, A Participatory Research Project: Denied Help! How Youth In The Sex Trade and Street Economy Are Turned Away From Systems Meant to Help Us & What We Are Doing to Fight Back*. These reports, particularly *Bad Encounter Line*, paved the way for the work we do today.
- **The National Council for Incarcerated and Formerly Incarcerated Women and Girls**, for their incredible and inclusive advocacy that has inspired and guided us.
- **Selene Means**, who took the stunning cover photo, capturing, the spirit of resilience and strength embodied in this work.

To the brave voices who shared their stories and wisdom, thank you for trusting us with your truths. Your courage is the foundation of this work.

To the staff and volunteers at COYOTE Rhode Island, your unwavering commitment to advocacy, harm reduction, mutual aid, and education continues to inspire us all. Your efforts are transforming lives and shaping a more just and compassionate society.

Special thanks to **SWOP Behind Bars**, whose leadership, vision, and relentless dedication have guided this project from inception to completion. Your advocacy for sex worker rights and your commitment to amplifying marginalized voices have made an indelible mark on this work and the movement as a whole.

To our collaborators, contributors, and supporters—your solidarity and generosity fuel this work. Thank you for believing in the power of community, storytelling, and activism.

Lastly, to the global community of sex workers and allies, this book is for you. May it serve as a beacon of resilience, empowerment, and hope.

In Solidarity,

Bella Robinson, Executive Director

COYOTERI

Introduction

This is a book of policy focused participatory action research (PAR) by and for sex workers and sex trafficking survivors in the United States.

The sex workers rights movement is first and foremost a workers' movement. Lawmakers and police create our working conditions, so they are the "bosses" that we turn to when negotiating for our labor and our safe work conditions. There are many books that delve into the history of prostitution regulation schemes in the United States and how they have affected sex workers as well as comparative research projects by groups like Amnesty International that examine sex workers' working conditions under various legal systems. This is the first book of participatory action research by and for people in the US sex industry.

Participatory action research is action research – research that aims to understand and solve a problem – that privileges the experience and knowledge of those closest to and most affected by the problem. PAR is done with and by, not on, the people most affected. It has roots in struggles for equality and has been used extensively in community development and solving workplace problems.

As a paradigm, PAR grounds the production of knowledge in real community needs and learning. When knowledge production about people in the sex industry is controlled by police and NGOs who profit from our criminalization, the information produced results in increased criminalization, which means no access to equal protection under criminal justice or labor protection laws - a state of danger for our community. When knowledge about us is produced by us, it is more relevant to our health and safety.

Because of criminalization, people in the sex industry are known as a hidden population – that is, researchers have a hard time finding us. The only effective way for researchers to find us is to partner with us: we know how to find each other. As an alternative, researchers have sometimes done research with incarcerated sex workers or sex workers in drug or alcohol treatment programs and often have padded their numbers by conflating all women who have ever traded a sexual favor for anything, even within the context of a committed relationship, with sex workers. This research does not reflect the entire community of sex workers, which is both broad and diverse.

As a hidden and criminalized population, sex workers do not often show up in the halls of our state capitals to advocate for our own health and safety. To do so would be to risk arrest and discrimination in housing, employment, child custody, and even banking. Sex worker activists who are willing to take these risks are few and far between. This means that research such as those found in this book is often the only way that the voices of people in the sex industry will reach lawmakers.

Throughout this book, we use the terms "sex workers" and "people in the sex industry" to refer broadly to all people in the sex industry. All of the research in this book includes people who meet legal definitions of sex trafficking survivors but who, for the most part, would not use that term to describe themselves. We respect their autonomy by not calling them sex trafficking survivors except in parts where their legal classification as such is an important part of understanding the data.

"Sex work" and "sex industry" refer to many kinds of work including phone sex, webcamming, adult content creation, pornography performers, strippers, kink providers, escorts, etc. While this book is focused on policy specifically surrounding prostitution, the largest research survey in this book did include other types of sex workers.

All of the sex workers who participated in these research projects bravely shared their knowledge and experience with the hopes that it would join with other sex workers' knowledge and experience and reach the lawmakers who so greatly impact our health and safety. We have done our best to quote the research participants as frequently as possible. Please give their experience and knowledge the consideration and respect they deserve.

Research Key

Name	Location	Participants	Year(s)	Chapter(s)
Alaska Survey	Alaska	48	2014	1, 7, 8
Rhode Island Survey	Rhode Island	63	2014-16	2, 7, 8
US Survey	United States	1515	2017	3, 4, 5, 6, 7, 8, 11
After FOSTA	United States	275	2018	9
Four Years of FOSTA	United States	248	2022	10
COVID-19	United States	189	2020	12

Each survey is introduced in the first chapter it appears in.

Chapter 1: People in Alaska's Sex Trade - Their Lived Experiences and Policy Recommendations

This chapter was written by Tara Burns, originally in 2014, as a summary of her master's thesis research at the University of Alaska Fairbanks.

Research Context

In 2012, a task force, a working group, and a round table were established to discuss prostitution and sex trafficking in Alaska. The task force and working group made recommendations that shaped Alaska's new sex trafficking law, passed in 2012. People with firsthand experience in Alaska's sex industry, including sex trafficking victims, were excluded from the groups and the process. Instead, the state turned to law enforcement and non-governmental organizations who profit from the criminalization of every aspect of prostitution.

The resulting law, passed in 2012, broadly redefined most adult consensual prostitution as sex trafficking. The only two people to be charged in the first two years of the laws existence were alleged prostitutes who were caught in ordinary prostitution stings and charged with facilitating or aiding prostitution (sex trafficking in the fourth degree) and felony sex trafficking charges like owning a place of prostitution (sex trafficking in the third degree) and receiving money from prostitution.

This legislation was followed by the creation of a statewide investigative unit targeting people in Alaska's sex trade and funding for conferences and prevention programs. On the other hand, I had received information from victims of force, fraud, and coercion within the sex industry that they were prosecuted for prostitution or trafficking themselves, and were regularly denied access to crisis shelter and counseling.

This research came from a desire to fully understand and quantify the effects of Alaska's sex trafficking and prostitution policies on all people in Alaska's sex trade. I was especially concerned about everyone in sex industry's ability to access equal protection under the law, health care, and emergency shelter. I wanted to know what was working, what wasn't working, and what they thought could work better.

The Research Ideology

Although sex workers and sex trafficking victims are constantly talked about in the media and public policy, stigma and criminalization often prevent them from speaking for themselves in media and legislative processes. As Alaska creates more and more policies that affect people in the sex trade, it becomes crucial to create a means for those impacted to bring their knowledge to the table. Participants' voices are foregrounded in this report because they have been so absent in other reports about sex trafficking and sex work in Alaska.

Rather than presenting participants in the context of their full lives, as is customary in social science research, I've done everything possible to protect their anonymity. That includes forgoing the use of pseudonyms and presenting some stories in pieces rather than with full context. All participation was voluntary and unpaid.

Methods

Surveys: Forty-one people who self-identified as having worked in Alaska's sex trade or having been profiled as a prostitute took the survey. One answered "erroneous data– please disregard" to all questions and was deleted, leaving 40 survey participants. The survey participants had from one to more than 31 years of experience in the sex trade, with the most common responses being 10 to 30 years. There was one male survey participant, and the rest were female. Participants were white, Alaska Native, Native American, Black, Latino, and Creole. There were no Asian participants.

Interviews: Seven people who had recently retired from Alaska's sex trade and one elder with significant knowledge of the history of prostitution and related policy in an Alaska Native community were interviewed. Interview participants were white, Alaska Native, Black, and Hispanic. They included a transgender person, an undocumented immigrant, formerly homeless youth, and people with graduate degrees. They had from 2 to 44 years in the sex trade and had worked as independent escorts, street-based workers, exotic dancers, massage parlor workers, and pornography performers and producers. They had worked in Asian massage parlors, and legal brothels. They had worked on a circuit, for pimps and agencies, made pornography, had survival sex as street-involved youth, and been pimped as a minor by a guardian. Four of them had significant experience and/or education in a helping profession. None of them thought of themselves as sex trafficking victims. According to an attorney who works with sex trafficking victims with whom I consulted, three definitely met the federal definition of a sex trafficking victim and one probably did.

Public Records: Indictments, affidavits, court transcripts, press releases, and more were examined to contextualize the experiences shared by participants.

Survey Demographics

- The average age of entry into prostitution was 19 years old (excluding one participant who didn't give a specific answer).

- The majority of participants had spent between 10 and 30 years in the industry.

- All had graduated from high school and 81% had pursued other education, ranging from advanced degrees to vocational schools.

- 48% entered the industry independently. Following entry, 89% went on to work independently in the industry.

- 7% reported being forced and 11% reported being coerced or manipulated when they entered the industry. 30% reported being coerced, manipulated, or forced at some point within the industry.

- 26% listed their age as less than 18 when they entered the industry.

Mobility within the Sex Industry

Participants reported substantial change in their working conditions within the sex industry. While a little less than half of the participants did not enter the industry working independently, about twice as many went on to work independently. These numbers are very similar to statistics reported in research done at John Jay College with youth in the sex trade, and echoes their conclusion that people in the sex trade have agency and act to change their situations.

Although only 18% of survey participants entered the industry being forced, coerced, or manipulated, an additional 12% went on to be coerced or manipulated in the industry. Participants reported being unable to go to the police when they were victimized in the industry and believed that lacking access to protection under the law made them vulnerable to predators.

What is Sex Trafficking?

It depends who you ask! According to popular opinion it might be an eight-year-old kidnapped and kept chained to a bed, or it might be everyone in the sex industry.

Under federal law, sex trafficking is (a) any minor working in the sex industry in any way or (b) the use of force, fraud, or coercion within the sex industry for financial profit.

Under Alaska state law all prostitution is framed as sex trafficking. In one case, a woman was charged with sex trafficking herself when the state alleged that she "instituted or aided" in her own prostitution.

The people who participated in this research are sex industry experts. None of them identify themselves as victims of sex trafficking. Thirty percent of the survey participants checked boxes that, under federal law, identify them as sex trafficking victims.

Seeking Shelter

The Numbers:

- 19% of survey participants had sought shelter.

- 83% of them were denied shelter.

- 50% of those who met the federal criteria for sex trafficking victims had sought shelter

- 100% of them were turned away.

Participant's Advice for Shelters:

"Don't discriminate"

"It shouldn't matter what we do for a living or where we met the person we need protection from"

"All people deserve a warm safe place to sleep, whether you approve of their choices or not."

"To educate staff about the realities for people involved in the sex trade. It is not helpful to judge nor to refuse services because you do not approve of other people's choices."

"Let them work"

How Do Shelters Interact with Sex Workers?

"They let me stay for a while and then I wasn't allowed to come back"

"I decided the streets offered more of a future"

"[They] said I wasn't the right kind of victim"

"[The shelter] wouldn't let me in when it was forty below, wouldn't give me shelter in general."

"I chose the streets over the shelter system, that was a very, very clear choice. I tried the shelters, I realized that I would not be able to maintain a place in that construct and so I chose going back out onto the streets [as a juvenile]."

Why Were So Many Unable to Access Shelter?

Survey participants did not offer much information about why they were unable to access shelter. Most seemed to feel that some discrimination was involved.

Since 2011, I've been aware of adults and minors (outside of this research) not being able to access shelter in Alaska because: they were underage and wouldn't give their parents' phone number (with good cause), they weren't willing to name the person who had trafficked them, they didn't have an ID, they were transgender, they were on felony probation, or they were victims of sex trafficking, not domestic violence.

The Sex Worker and the Force of Law

Sex workers reported an alarming amount of police violence. When they tried to report being a victim or witness of a crime, most of their reports were not taken; some were arrested or threatened with arrest when they had been the victim or witness of a crime. In the interviews, 75% percent of those who meet the federal definition of a sex trafficking victim reported being assaulted by police before ever becoming involved in the sex industry, compared to 0% of those who did not have trafficking experiences.

The Numbers:

- 52% of participants had tried to report being a victim or witness of a crime while working

- The police took 44% of their reports. They arrested 6% of them and threatened 33% with arrest when they were trying to report being the victim or witness of a crime.

- 80% of participants who had been manipulated or coerced in the industry had tried to report being a victim or witness of a crime. When they did, the police took 20% of their reports, threatened 60% with arrest, and arrested 20%.

- 74% of participants had been a victim or witness of a crime that they didn't report because they thought they would be arrested, they didn't think the police would do anything, they didn't want to draw attention to themselves or their coworkers, or other reasons.

- 26% of participants had been sexually assaulted by an officer.

- 60% of those who had been coerced or manipulated and 50% of those who had been forced had been sexually assaulted by an officer.

- 9% of participants had been robbed or beaten by an officer.

- 40% of those who had been coerced or manipulated in the industry and 50% of those who had been forced had been robbed or beaten by an officer.

- 56% of those who tried to report a crime to the police did not have their reports taken:

"I have a friend that was walking on Spenard a couple years ago and a guy in a truck had raped her and she already knew who it was and she reported it to the police. Other girls had reported the same thing happening and he's still driving around doing what he does… They ignored her. They didn't do anything at all. I don't know the specific details but I know that she was really frustrated about it and she didn't feel safe at all."

- 74% of survey participants indicated that they had been the victim or witness of a crime they had not reported. 39% didn't believe the police would do anything, and 30% believed they would be arrested if they tried to report.

Firsthand Experiences:

"I myself have had them pose as customers and actually complete a sexual act with me and then try to arrest me however I didn't touch the money so they couldn't arrest me and, um… I felt raped after. Completely raped."

"When I was a kid I was in a park with a friend of mine, yeah we were underage and drinking beer in the park which we shouldn't have been doing, but they beat my friend into a coma."

"She came to my house in handcuffs, I helped cut her out of handcuffs. She got away from a policeman who was going – he threatened to throw her in the [river] if she didn't perform oral sex on him."

"They always treat you like you're stupid, that you must have a pimp, you must be on drugs, that you need to get a job. This is my job. Let's see what else… Um, it's never been a good encounter but I've never experienced violence or sexual harassment. Thankfully."

"Just from what I've heard from everybody else, that if something bad was to happen to not trust law enforcement to carry out any justice. You know that's why it's so important these days to communicate with others that are in the field so you can know who the client is. I mean, if I were looking to screen a client I wouldn't look to make sure they're not law enforcement, I'd make sure that they're not, you know, domestic violence, that they haven't racked up a bunch of assaults and robberies, they don't have any weird drug charges or kidnapping charges and make sure that it's a safe environment, because I know that if it wasn't I couldn't just call the police and know that everything would be okay. I couldn't call the police and be treated like a typical public person."

"I ended up going to a girls' home from 13 to 14 and, we were bad kids, we tried to escape, they ended up beating us up and throwing us in solitary confinement until our bruises healed so then nobody could see that and nobody would believe us because we were bad kids."

"It was in the middle of the day. I was walking by the police, I was walking to catch a bus. And because I was in the area that I was in and I had an acid wash miniskirt on and a little tank top, they wanted to see whether or not I was, I was trans. And they ripped my underwear off. One of them put his hand up my skirt and ripped my underwear off. He slammed me down on the car, he injured me. Um, left me with some broken fingertips, broken toes, fractured cheekbone. And they felt perfectly okay with this because there was no law to protect me...

'I mean, when you deny a certain group of people their protections or rights, or say... you're saying that it's okay to abuse these people. I mean, you set a precedent. You know what I'm saying? You set a precedent. I mean, there are plenty of people that hate Black people, but they would never act on it because it's against the law to discriminate and it's against the law to harm them now. So therefore people who would harm them or discriminate against them keep that under wraps because they know there's laws against it and there's consequences. These officers didn't feel like there was any consequences to doing that. They left me there in a 7/11 parking lot. I was bleeding, I had my skirt ripped. I basically looked like a rape victim or an assault victim and people were just mortified because they'd seen a teenage girl get assaulted by a police officer, two police officers. And yeah, these guys didn't feel like there was any consequences."

"[In the 90's I] went to the FBI in Manhattan and I reported part of a syndicate after I was beaten up and given a bad check from the legal company that was a front for

illegal activity. There were some things building to that, but the reason that I was beaten up was because the workers were locked in on a premise and we needed to get supplies because the house was selling our supplies at like 100% markup and all of the workers needed supplies and I was voted as being the person who had the most self-confidence and ability to try to communicate that, and it ended up with me being beaten up and potentially put into it an even more detrimental situation. I had to think about that long and hard because other people supported my doing it. The problem at that point was that it would take a hundred calls to vice and in an area of the country each from separate people who all were willing to identify themselves with their full legal name, and until there were 100 complaints put in an investigation could not be opened up. And if anything happened to you at that point in time if you were a hooker or defined as an aberrant of any kind you would get a stamp on your file that said that you were not a human investigation. The NHI stamp was for people who were sex workers, drug pushers, gang people, and if you got offed there was no investigation. So there was a lot there…

All of my contact with law enforcement has been so ridiculously clearly defined by what their present administrative goal directive is as opposed to what the actual needs of people are that you realize that you have to understand more about what's going on from the national and state perspective politically before you go to the police. It's not about a crime or a moral code or ethics, it's about the political framework, the contextual framework, the political structure of the administration that is existent in the time that you are potentially experiencing a problem.

That's not how law enforcement is defined to you when you're a child but now I get that. So, you know, if you see something bad happening you have to take into consideration whether or not the time period, the belief of the time period that you're in, is going to wind up understanding the nature of the crime.

I realize now that it wasn't ridiculous that I went to the FBI but it was ridiculous that I would believe that anybody would care if there was no money attached to them caring about something. There has to be like some kind of cookie that they're getting."

It Is Not Illegal in Alaska for Police Officers to Have Sex with People Before Arresting Them:

"I knew a couple ladies who went to go see a guy together who turned out to be a police officer. He gave one of the girls that was only 19 at the time alcohol. He also received oral sex from one of the ladies and then arrested her and said that he had seen her reviews online and wanted to see for himself what it was all about. She got a prosti-tution charge."

"I know another lady who went to see someone who was supposed to be a customer who ended up being a police officer and they had sex to completion. He tried to make her take the money but she did not take the money. He told her he was going to arrest her and she informed him that he couldn't because they had not broken any law. He then proceeded to say, "You're a very wise woman and I'm proud of you," and proceeded to walk her downstairs where

Force, Manipulation, Underage Work, and Police Violence

I compared the responses of people who reported experiencing force or manipulation within the sex industry and those who reported working underage (the federal standard for sex trafficking) with the general survey results. Those who had experienced force or manipulation within the industry were completely unable to access shelter, and reported a much higher rate of sexual assault, physical assault, and robbery by police officers. There didn't seem to be a difference in their ability to access medical or mental health care. Working underage didn't seem to be related to significant differences.

I compared people who reported having been assaulted by police to those who had not, and found some differences. Of the two people who had been beaten or robbed by an officer:

- Both were both white and Alaska Native.

- Both reported entering the industry using sex for survival.

- Neither entered the industry working independently but both went on to work independently.

- Reported that criminal history and lack of job history would have made it difficult for them to leave the industry if they'd wanted to.

- Both had sought emergency shelter, in both cases the shelter was aware of their involvement in the industry, and both were ultimately unable to access shelter.

- Both had tried to report being a victim or witness of a crime, police took one of their reports and threatened both with arrest.

- Both reported having been the victim or witness of a crime they didn't report because they didn't think the police would do anything and they thought they would be arrested.

- Both had been arrested as adults, and both had been detained but not arrested as adults.

- Both believed police are the primary threat to people in Alaska's sex industry.

Of those who reported being sexually assaulted by an officer:

- Half were Alaska Native and white, the other half were white.

- None entered the industry working independently. Following entry, all went on to work independently.

- Half had sought emergency shelter; none were able to access it.

- 93% reported being a victim or witness of a crime they didn't report.

- All but one believed police are the primary threat to people in Alaska's sex industry.

The Sex Trafficking Laws

- Alleged prostitutes charged with trafficking: 3

- Non- prostitutes charged with trafficking: 3

- "Traffickers" charged with hurting prostitutes: 0

- "Traffickers" charged with pimping children: 0

When I was first considering conducting this research, I made a public records request to find out how the sex trafficking statutes in Alaska had been used since its inception. That was at the end of 2013, and at that time only two people had been charged with sex trafficking. Both women were allegedly prostitutes who were charged with sex trafficking in the same cases that they were charged with prostitution of themselves. In one case the woman was charged with trafficking herself ("facilitating or aiding prostitution") after she refused to agree to perform a sex act with an undercover police officer for money. In the other case a woman was charged with multiple counts of felony sex trafficking (maintaining a place of prostitution, receiving money from prostitution, etc) for sharing space with other sex workers when she booked a duo for herself and another worker with a police officer. The only people charged with prostitution under state law at that time were those who were also charged with sex trafficking and those who were allegedly victims of sex trafficking.

Since that records request, four more people have been charged with sex trafficking. One is a woman who, in the charging documents, is accused of being a prostitute. Another is her husband, who is charged with receiving money from prostitution. The other two are men who are accused of maintaining places of prostitution and receiving money from prostitution. There have been no charges of violence, fraud, or coercion in any of the cases. In one case there was originally an allegation of a verbal threat, but that charge was later dropped. In none of the documents I've examined since the law's inception has it been used to benefit a victim.

There is a big gap between the federal definition of sex trafficking, which involves either minors or the use of force, fraud, or coercion, and the state definition of sex trafficking, which includes many strategies that sex workers employ to increase their safety, such as working indoors, working together, and facilitating or aiding their own prostitution.

What Are the Real Risks to People in Alaska's Sex Trade?

"So many at this point. You know we can't, we're not supposed to get together, we're not supposed to talk about how to keep each other safe, we're not supposed to share spaces, we're not supposed to, you know, help with references or any-thing like that because we're worried about being arrested. So... and then not only that but people know that they can harm you and get away with it because you can't go to the police because you'll be arrested right with them. So you'll be victimized twice."

"You can't really be honest on applications for loans or anything. Mainly, I mean, there is risk when you go to an

outcall and what if there's guys hiding in a closet? You can't just finally make it out of there and call the police and say I was raped without questions, "Oh, well she's a prostitute" and then your labeled, maybe charged, and those guys aren't."

I asked people in Alaska's sex trade what the primary threats that the law should be concerned with protecting them from are. In the survey:

- 35% named violence or coercion from police

- 30% mentioned not being able to access equal protection under the law if they were the victim of a crime

- 15% mentioned arrest or prosecution (things that can result in lifelong discrimination in accessing employment, housing, custody, education, social services, and financial instruments)

What Should Be the Definition of Sex Trafficking?

Overwhelmingly participants thought sex trafficking should be defined as when someone was forced or coerced against their will to perform acts of prostitution. Many thought that most force, fraud, or coercion that happens in the industry would more properly be described and charged as domestic violence, assault, or labor abuses.

How Common Is Sex Trafficking, According to the Different Definitions?

- 71% of survey participants thought that sex trafficking, according to their own definition, happens never or sometimes in Alaska.

- 85% thought that sex trafficking, according to federal definitions, happens never or some-times in Alaska.

- 73% thought that sex trafficking, according to state law, happens most or all of the time.

What Should Be the Difference Between Prostitution and Sex Trafficking?

"When it's not by choice of the individual. An individual should come forward to you. just as if, there are some, like, places in the southwest, they're like, cutting up chickens and stuff. Right, some of these big places. And they kidnap people from like Mexico and Central America and crap. They literally just kidnap them and enslave them and bring them up here to, like, pick tomatoes or whatever, horrible jobs. And that's the same thing, it's taking someone and enslaving them into prostitution. you don't take someone and force them to do anything that's not by their choice. That's slavery. That's illegal. You don't do it."

"But if I wake up in morning and I make my breakfast and I make myself a beautiful breakfast every morning, I make myself a beautiful paleo diet breakfast, I have a mineral sparkling water and take my phone calls and my emails, and I set up a few appointments with some gentleman that I enjoy spending time with, and they pay me for that time, those two should not be considered the same thing. At all. It needs to stop."

"The oldest profession in the world is prostitution. Sex trafficking to me is such a vile term, because that's just sadness, I mean when someone's being forced to do something that they don't want to do against their will, that's just horrible and I would definitely help somebody get out of that situation even if it put me at risk just because we're human and I wouldn't wanna see someone treated like that. But, you know I think there's a big difference between doing it because you want to and doing it because you're forced to."

"I think they need to change the definition of sex trafficking, it's a really bad definition. The whole trafficking definition and discourses is a bad discourse. I mean we don't talk about labor trafficking in terms of, you know, construction trafficking. We don't talk about trafficking or exploitation in industries specific to those industries and so singling out, you know, the sex trade when we're already being exploited by the criminalization laws is an unfair business practice, actually is what it is. They need to remove, um, they need to remove all the sex trafficking laws specifically and they need to instead strengthen labor laws and make them actually enforceable because most of the labor laws on the books are not enforceable. Well the only way that they're actually enforceable is if you go and have the means to hire your own private attorney to seek damages so… that's not a fair equitable way to prevent. Laws have to be built around prevention not around prosecution of crimes that already happen after the fact, that's totally useless."

"Prostitution is consensual amongst adults. It is a negotiated understanding of time and action to dollar amount so that mutual expectations are satisfied. Trafficking - people in my view are either forced or coerced to work with the terms not being clear with the financial aspects not being fairly negotiated or implemented and their needs, whether that be healthcare or food, not met within the construct of the transaction. And sometimes trafficking can be agreed to because people don't feel they have other options so it's not always—like sometimes people agree to things that are beyond their understanding—but basically when you start taking a clear parameter of time, place, service offered, you don't offer people clean hygienic places to eat, bathe, sleep, and [they don't] understand what they're in for."

What Laws Would Serve People in the Sex Industry?

Survey participants gave short answers: most people thought that decriminalization is the answer, particularly decriminalizing prostitutes working together, working indoors (in *"places of prostitution"*), sharing information with each other about clients, and having drivers. Others mentioned things like, "if [sex workers] could go to the police without being arrested," and "consequences and public shaming for cops who take advantage of their power to get free sex from us."

Interview participants had a lot more to say:

"I will say that maybe there is a need for there to be some kind of advocate-liaison that works between sex workers and law enforcement… If you have a sex worker who has been taken into custody either voluntarily or in some kind

47

of a raid or situation, if they are able to have an advocate present—who hasn't just gotten a degree, but truly understands the industry from both an experiential and an academic perspective— to be there to help make sure the situation is correctly, uh transcribed or recorded, or that the rights of the person are clearly, like, that their situation, that their rights are clearly understood or any rights they're giving away are clearly understood. There aren't any lawyers that are sex industry specific and that's a problem. So whether it be having you know, these task forces, find people in the sex industry and pay for them to do you like the combination of a counsel and legal program to then be able to act as these interdisciplinary liaisons, because there's no there's no buffer, there's no objective buffer that I see."

"Oh, decriminalization. Decriminalization would go a long way to doing that [ending violence] because if they are, if these transactions are occurring through legitimate means then clients don't feel like they necessarily… you know, again there's that invisible barrier of, it's the law and if I cross over this barrier and do something I'm not supposed to do there's going to be consequences, whereas when it is a criminal act and this client is feeling like this lady, the lady or gentleman that he's getting services from hasn't any recourse then he might feel a little more okay about doing whatever [to the sex worker]."

"It would be nice for the police not to victimize people that are victimized themselves and just because we're in this business doesn't mean that we're victims. I see myself maybe only made a victim, maybe only if somebody was to

do something to me and then as a tax-paying individual because I pay my taxes, that the police don't do anything about it, then I'm a victim on both ends."

"Oh yeah, I mean in a perfect world, my perfect world, this would be legal and then when there was somebody that was working that felt like they were being mistreated or the guys take all the money they would actually be able to reach out and get out of that situation without being labeled as a prostitute or labeled as a lost cause or drug addict or someone who's just screwed up in the head."

"Stop pursuing us like hunted animals… If you stop pursuing the criminalization of prostitution, then I can come to you when I'm raped, then I can come to you when I'm robbed, then you can pursue violent crimes."

"If consensual prostitution amongst adults who are mutually in agreement of wanting to engage in a situation was decriminalized. I think, you know, either [in] a private in-house situation or an outcall situation or combination of, but if consensual adult to adult prostitution was decriminalized then right there, there would be a platform for feeling more secure, with an ability to communicate if you see bad things happening to other people, or if you have a bad experience yourself, whether that be with a client who is violent or abberated or just really creepy or a house that is not acting ethically."

"You are more inclined to also if you are in a decriminalized situation and there is a healthcare clinic that will see people who are in the sex industry just as there are GLBT [sic] specific healthcare clinics that have a grant

structure to be able to allow people to receive services, treatment, testing treatment, and counsel for behavior related to homosexual relations. If there were something like that for sex workers where you could be honest about whether or not you use condoms for oral sex, vaginal sex, anal sex and wanted to have testing done for STI's HIV, or if you're feeling burnt out and you needed to have just acute counsel or you know, kind of a grounding session so to speak to prevent volatile situations where often people reach out for drugs and alcohol if they don't have people who can help soothe and ground them. If you have places to go where you can communicate honestly without being punished for that sometimes that can prevent an escalation of volatile and negative situations right there. And also that way you can track healthcare issues in an area."

"But decriminalization in my mind is definitely the starting point for that. The other thing is that that way - if there are people who are minors or who are obviously not mentally or physically competent to be working, that those agencies that are support systems to the industry can help get those people out of work situations and get the resources they need. If somebody is obviously [mentally ill] or they are suffering from a drug problem or they're homeless and malnourished and they really shouldn't be working. If you can refer them to places that can help them get some of the resources they need to help get them out of the work environment. That way workers don't have to - actual sex workers don't have to work with people who are not necessarily meant or able to be working."

Summary of Recommendations

1. Institute immediate external oversight of all interactions between police and those they believe to be sex workers or sex trafficking victims in order to prevent police misconduct, including sexual misconduct and the failure on the part of police to properly take and investigate reports.

2. Institute regular accountability procedures for shelters and rape crisis centers to ensure that all victims have access to services. As shown in this report, the arbitrary selection of who is "deserving" of services negatively impacts the most vulnerable among us.

3. Decriminalize prostitution so that sex workers, sex trafficking victims, and their customers can report crime without fear of arrest.

4. Repeal Alaska's sex trafficking law.

5. Consult those in the sex industry before making new laws to prevent the dangerous effects that participants have reported.

6. Immediately discontinue the use of safety measures as evidence of prostitution or against alleged prostitutes or their clients. Safety measures include condoms, negotiating safer sex, screening, working indoors (in a "place of prostitution"), working together, and hiring someone to do security, screening, or booking. Making sex workers afraid to use condoms or screen clients should not be a goal or effect of prostitution policy.

7. Shelters and other service providers should institute non-discrimination policies and seek training from sex workers

8. Develop policy and procedures that support minors seeking shelter and other services. Minors should never be turned away from shelters because their situations are too complex or because it would endanger them to contact their guardians.

9. Establish criminal penalties for police who have sexual contact with sex workers or sex trafficking victims.

10. Investigate the relationship between police violence and abuse within the sex industry and use this to guide policy going forward.

Chapter 2: Policing Modern-Day Slavery in RI

"Stop persecuting us, and don't go after clients who've behaved themselves, Stop raping sex workers. Stop blaming victims. Stop letting actual criminals who target sex workers BECAUSE they are vulnerable to get away with crimes."

Survey Participant

Key Findings

- 47% of sex workers surveyed said they had been the victim or witness of a crime they did not report to police.

- 79% of those who had reported a crime to police said that their reports weren't taken, 6% said they were arrested, and 21% were threatened with arrest when trying to report a crime.

- 11% said a police officer had coerced them into giving them free sex, and 15% said they had been robbed or assaulted by a police officer.

Background

The impetus for this research project was when Tara Burns came to give a lecture in Rhode Island in 2014 on similar work she had carried out in Alaska. Her project, which is outlined in the chapter before this one, provided new insights into how we can conceptualize trafficking victims and how sex workers perceive themselves. Tara generously allowed COYOTE RI to adapt some of her research questions on sex work. We asked these questions to gauge how sex workers reviewed their relationships with institutions. This would allow us to gain a more comprehensive understanding of sex workers and what services they require. Therefore, this chapter will provide an overview of statistics on sex workers in Rhode Island.

The type of statistics we use here are descriptive. This means that they show a broad overview of a population. They are meant to help us understand who sex workers are despite stereotypes that we have heard before. Additionally, much writing on sex workers that exists is anecdotal or relies on reports from a few case studies that may not represent most people. By giving a broad, quantitative overview of sex workers we can contribute to the current knowledge base. We have supplemented these statistics with qualitative interview questions. Qualitative questions are open-ended and allow people to answer in their own words. We can look for patterns in the answers to help us understand some of the more complex questions about sex work.

We hope that this book will complement academic material such as reports by esteemed organizations including Amnesty International, UN AIDS, ACLU, and Lancet HIV that advocate for the decriminalization of sex work to improve sex workers' health and safety. Additionally, we hope that lawmakers, social service providers, and other people who can impact sex worker safety will read this work and listen to our perspectives. For many involved in the industry, policy surrounding sex work is a matter of life and death.

Research Context: Rhode Island

Our work has centered in Rhode Island (RI). Sex work in RI is currently illegal. However, from 2003 to 2009 the state briefly and inadvertently decriminalized sex work through a district court decision. The origin of decriminalization was in a 1976 lawsuit, COYOTE v. Roberts. The local chapter of COYOTE sued the Attorney General of Rhode Island and Chief of Police of the City of Providence, arguing that the state statute prohibiting prostitution was unconstitutional and overly broad. In 1980, the RI state legislature amended language related to that specific statute changing solicitation to a misdemeanor and removing language referring to prostitution as a crime. Legislators claimed that this connection between the lawsuit and the language change was coincidental and that they were not trying to legalize sex work. In 1998, the Rhode Island State Supreme Court ruled in State v. DeMagistris that the law criminalizing prostitution was "primarily to bar prostitutes from hawking their wares in public," and that someone who engages in sex work privately could not be prosecuted under this law.

In 2003, the case Rhode Island ex rel. City of Providence v. Choe enshrined protections for indoor sex workers. From 2003 to 2009, RI briefly saw the complete decriminalization of sex work for workers who were based indoors. After many attempts, proponents of criminalization finally passed legislation in 2009. The passage of re-criminalization laws was led largely by "anti-trafficking" movement supporters including academics, religious leaders, and people profiting from anti-trafficking "rescue" services. Many of these relied on "research" that prioritized the perspectives of law enforcement officers and social service providers. These ignored the perspectives of sex workers themselves.

One aspect of RI's period of decriminalization was that it created an environment for "natural experiments." This is a term used by many scientists to refer to a study in which different groups (experiment or non-experiment) are determined by nature. What this meant is that it made it easier for scientists like economists to see how sex work decriminalization affected people in a real-world environment. For example, economists such as Scott Cunningham & Manisha Shah (2017) have explored how decriminalization affected outcomes such as STI prevalence and violence. They showed that the era of decriminalization was associated with a 30% decrease in rape reports and a 40% decrease in gonorrhea with all else held equal.

We aimed to build on preliminary work on how sex work decriminalization affected health outcomes. To our knowledge, this is the most comprehensive work on sex worker perspectives in Rhode Island shortly following the re-criminalization of sex work. The intention of this study was to survey sex workers who were working in the industry in the context of post-decriminalization. This meant that most sex workers involved in the survey would have either known about or experienced decriminalization themselves. Many sex workers explicitly referred to their time working in an atmosphere where sex work was decriminalized, adding richness to the survey results.

Methods

We conducted a survey of 63 sex workers living in Rhode Island from 2014 to 2016. The study was co-sponsored between COYOTE-RI and the Brown University Center for the Study of Slavery & Justice. The goal of the study was to measure the effects of the 2009 decision to return to criminalization in Rhode Island,

and it was funded by an American Sociological Association Community Action Research Initiative grant. We recruited participants through respondent-driven sampling. After initially sharing the survey on Backpage, a website used by sex workers to sell services, we used referrals to other participants to gauge replies from a diverse sample. A major strength of this study is its novelty.

We asked 40 questions, which included demographics (such as gender, race, education), experiences with police, age of entry into sex work, experiences with reporting violence, housing, and experience access services such as mental health and aid. We also asked questions about knowledge of federal and local sex trafficking laws, as well as their personal definitions of trafficking. We were interested in finding out if sex workers perceived themselves as victims, as well as how we could prevent minors from entering the sex industry.

We also asked what barriers sex workers faced to exiting the industry as well as risks for sex workers. We were curious about how sex workers navigated barriers such as forced work, fraud, and coercion.

Results

Demographics

Most participants (94%) were female, and 3% (n=2) were transgender. Almost all (n=62) participants had completed at least a high school degree, and 43% had an advanced degree. The sample was 87% white, which is reflective of Rhode Island demographics. The first age at which participants had traded sex for anything of value ranged from 14-50, with 86% being 18 or older. This challenges many previous statistics used by the anti-trafficking industry. For instance, some have purported that the average age of entry is as low as 13 based on unclear methodology. This claim was not reflected in our research.

Relationships with Law Enforcement

We found that many sex workers in Rhode Island were fearful of law enforcement. Many reported previous negative experiences with the police. Horrifyingly, 47% of sex workers reported that they had been the victim or witness of a crime they did not report to the police. When asked why they did not report, 27% responded that they did not report because they didn't think the police would do anything, while 32% did not report because they didn't want to draw attention to their co-workers because of perceived illegal activity. This is a disaster for public safety.

Of those who did report a crime to police, 79% noted that the police did not take their report. Additionally, 6% were arrested while trying to report a crime and 21% reported being threatened with arrest by the police when trying to report a crime. None of the respondents who had been threatened with arrest had been asked by police if they were being coerced into sex work.

About half (53%) of respondents had reported some other type of contact with the police during their time in the sex industry. Some of these participants (15%) were robbed or assaulted by a police officer and 11% reported that a police officer had collected a "freebie" (using the threat of arrest to coerce the women into providing them a free sex act). Additionally, 35% of the sample had been arrested as either an adult or a minor. Of the participants who had been arrested, 42% had been charged with prostitution.

We explored whether the police had provided any helpful services with qualitative questions. One participant stated, "I think many police understand what sex workers are dealing with but they also have to obey laws so most are probably torn between what is right and the laws in place."

Most participants did not feel they could report crimes to or expect help from police. Some described past traumatizing interactions with police officers such as one participant who stated:

> *"I was in my early 20`s, pulled over and was offered a free "go" on a [driving under the influence] charge if I [gave the officer oral sex], I refused and got a [driving under the influence charge] [Later] a police officer asked me invasive questions and photographed me. My interactions are never good with police."*

Another participant responded that she had been arrested after reporting a client who she perceived as dangerous. She reported that she was not allowed to dress during her arrest:

> *"A client turned me in after I refused to see him because he was rough. I was charged with solicitation and offered diversion. The police would not let me dress. I was forced to sit in lingerie as they questioned me and searched the house. It was the most humiliating experience of my life."*

Another participant described a raid following law enforcement's discovery of her online advertising:

> *"They kicked in the door to my home without a warrant, waving guns around and screaming 'we know what is going on here' because I had an online escort ad. This was the*

most traumatic event of my life and it has left me with PTSD."

Only one participant reported a fairly positive experience with the police:

"[Police] were very friendly to me. They told me I didn't "look the type". They did not handcuff me. They booked me and drove me back to my in-call [...] They tried to drop the charges, but the media had already gotten ahold of it. [media outlets continued to question the District Attorney about the pending charges in the case]"

We also asked if sex workers had any suggestions for law enforcement in how to best serve and protect people in the sex industry. Most discussed how law enforcement officers should de-prioritize the arrest of workers providing consensual services. For instance, a participant responded:

"Focus on cases where the woman/worker is in actual danger, protect the anonymity of workers, do not assume all workers are trafficked."

Another stated:

"Sex workers want to forge relationships with local law enforcement, and we want "equal protection" under the law, and we want the ability to report violence and possible trafficking tips to the police."

While some participants reported neutral attitudes toward or interactions with law enforcement, the majority were fearful of policing and many reported past negative experiences that they perceived as deterring their ability to report crimes.

Experiences Seeking Social Services

We additionally asked about interactions with social service providers. Overall, 19% of sex workers who responded to the survey had sought out shelter services, 85% medical services, 48% mental health services, and 33% legal aid.

Of those who sought shelter services, 85% did not disclose their involvement in the sex industry to shelter staff. When asked how shelters could better accommodate people involved in the sex industry, one participant stated that she had a negative experience after she was outed as a sex worker:

> *"I was treated OK at the DV [Domestic Violence] shelter until someone recognized me from my backpage ad. I was treated horribly after that, and I was told that I should try going to another shelter because they claimed me being there was upsetting the other women. I was not kicked out but after a few days of listening to hateful gossip, I thought going back to my abusive boyfriend might be better than staying where I was not wanted."*

Another participant discussed how she had difficulty receiving services because as a transgender woman she was not allowed to stay in an all-female facility. These considerations are important for sex workers given the high prevalence of transgender sex workers who suffer from a "double disadvantage" in stigma based on both their gender identity and their experience working in a stigmatized industry.

Some participants discussed that they feared mistreatment from medical providers upon disclosure of their experiences selling sexual services. They were consequently unable to communicate relevant information related to their health status.

Additionally, some mentioned that they perceived medical spaces as safe spaces for treatment yet had experiences with mistrust. For example, one participant described reporting rape at the hospital:

> *"The hospital staff at the ER were very nice until the police showed up to take my report and once they found out I was an escort they told me that if I wanted to press charges against the man who raped me, that I would be arrested for prostitution. At this point, the hospital staff got cold distant and some of them became downright rude to me."*

We asked how medical providers could better respond to the needs of people in the sex industry. They communicated a need for health providers to understand how stigma operates and how it can impede receiving services for people involved in the sex industry.

Some participants also had negative experiences in seeking mental health treatment. They stated that they had been urged to leave the industry or had perceived judgment for their occupation. When asked how mental health professionals could better understand the needs of people in the sex industry, one sex worker recommended that "mental health professionals should know that they do not have to talk people out of being in the industry but they do need to understand the industry so they can support sex workers properly."

Trafficking Perceptions

When asked if participants knew anyone who worked in prostitution under conditions of force, fraud, or coercion or were under 18, most (81%) participants stated that they did not know anyone who met this definition. However, 14% stated that they knew 1-2 people who they felt matched this definition. Most participants (52%) perceived that sex trafficking rarely happened in Rhode Island, 36% stated that it happened sometimes, two respondents reported that it never happened, and one stated that it happened a lot of the time or all of the time. When asked who they felt would be at the highest risk for being trafficked, participants cited underserved populations such as migrants, homeless individuals, people who use drugs, members of the LGBTQ community, and minors.

Participants responded to the question "What do you think could be done to prevent people from being frauded or coerced into working for another person's profit?" with a range of suggestions. Many recommended the decriminalization of sex work, providing more services to people experiencing poverty, better mental health infrastructure, and support services for minors and people who were members of vulnerable communities. They emphasized real risks to sex workers such as dangerous clients, threats from law enforcement, exploitation, robbery, and rape that were exacerbated by criminalization. For instance, one participant suggested:

> *"Stop persecuting us, and don't go after clients who've behaved themselves, Stop raping sex workers. Stop blaming victims. Stop letting actual criminals who target sex workers BECAUSE they are vulnerable to get away with crimes."*

Many respondents emphasized decriminalization as a way to reduce trafficking, such as a worker who commented that laws against exploitation already existed without the criminalization of sex work:

"If it were decriminalized, normal laws already in place would protect sex workers from crimes." Others emphasized that sex workers themselves had lived experience in the industry and should be included in policy decisions pertaining to their safety and purchasing dynamics: " Sex workers could be the best tool that law enforcement has in the fight against trafficking. Sex workers need to be included in all legislation [and] policies that impact their lives."

Leaving the industry

Many stated that barriers to leaving sex work included lack of employment opportunities, low wages in other industries, and the inability to report previous work experience due to the stigma associated with being a sex worker. Some discussed how decriminalization could make it more feasible for workers who wanted to leave the industry to exit. One participant stated:

"First of all, it is hard to get out of it, if you are making good money. Second of all, you have to ask yourself questions if you really want to do this for the rest of your life. Lack of legitimate work history makes it hard to get a job outside of the industry, [and] once [you're] convicted of being a prostitute life will never be the same again, arrest records make it almost impossible to leave. Decriminalization would go a long way towards making options for exit better."

The difficulties in exiting the industry were especially pronounced for those who had been convicted of a prostitution-related offense, such as a respondent who expressed:

"I think my past prostitution conviction would stop me from landing a good job, this is one of the reasons, I have not bothered going to college and getting my degree, because the world will see me like a whore, so why bother?"

Conclusion

Participants in Rhode Island discussed ways in which past experiences had contributed to the aversion to service seeking and fear of reporting crimes to law enforcement. Many also discussed how criminalization contributed to opportunistic crimes against sex workers who were considered vulnerable because their profession was not legal. Participants discussed a normalization of violence against sex workers and stigma that impeded their ability to flourish.

Policy Insights

We recommend that:

- Social service providers incorporate more sex worker-led training on experiences with stigma.

- That sex workers are incorporated into policy decisions that affect their lives.

- That law enforcement prioritizes violence against sex workers over arrest and harassment of workers.

Chapter 3: US Survey: Demographics

"Sex workers need to be included in all legislation [and] policies that impact their lives."

Survey Participant

Key Findings

- The average age of sex workers surveyed was 33.

- Our data reflect mostly cisgender white women and US citizens' experiences.

- Many respondents were LGBTQ+; only 37% identified as straight.

- An overwhelming majority of sex workers tend to have at least a high school degree; many had additional education or training.

- Some sex workers experienced some form of out-of-home care (like foster care or a juvenile justice placement) during childhood, but the majority did not.

Introduction

This chapter will provide an overview of the characteristics of sex workers in the United States. We conducted the most comprehensive survey to our knowledge on sex worker demographics and experiences. Sex workers' opinions and experiences have often been omitted by policymakers and academics. Our research was only able to locate one other national survey of sex workers previously conducted in the U.S., which focused on questions related to workers' perception of sex trafficking prevalence.[1] COYOTE's survey included questions to learn how sex workers keep themselves safe, and what a world that recognizes their rights would look like to them. This was a community-based project; our knowledge base is from sex workers themselves. This chapter will describe this project and our methods.

In this chapter, we will talk about the findings from this survey. We hope this book will be useful to community organizations and policymakers. Further chapters will describe family relationships, past and current labor history, trafficking, violence, arrests, accessing public services, and HIV and sexual health. We will conclude with recommendations for public groups.

Overall, our sample was mostly white and female. Participants mostly self-described as LGBTQ+, with only 37% identifying as straight. They were also highly educated with most possessing at least a high school degree and many having further education. The average age was 33, and the average length of time in the industry was 7 years.

Methods

This research was conducted in collaboration with Coyote Rhode Island (RI), Desiree Alliance, SWOP Behind Bars, and The Center for the Study of Slavery and Justice at Brown University, who all collaborated on the survey design. The survey included 145

---

[1] Jessica Bishop-Royse, Danielle Bastian, Crysta Heart & Greg Scott (2021). "Trafficking in the Erotic Labor Market: A National Survey." Journal of Human Trafficking, 7(2): 121-136.

questions on demographics, relationships, labor history, and safety practices. The questions elicited both quantitative and qualitative data. The survey was open for 3 months in the summer of 2017. We spent hundreds of hours emailing sex worker advertisers and reached out to partner organizations to share the survey online and through their community networks to gain a wide reach of participants, eventually totaling 1515 participants. This is only the second national survey of sex workers to ever have been conducted, the first to be conducted by a sex-worker led organization themselves, and the largest survey of US sex workers to have ever been done.

Demographics

The survey reached most geographic regions in the United States evenly. Of all respondents, 12% were from the Northeast, 14% were from the mid-Atlantic, 15% were from the Southeast, 13% were from the Southwest, 18% were from the West, 9% were from

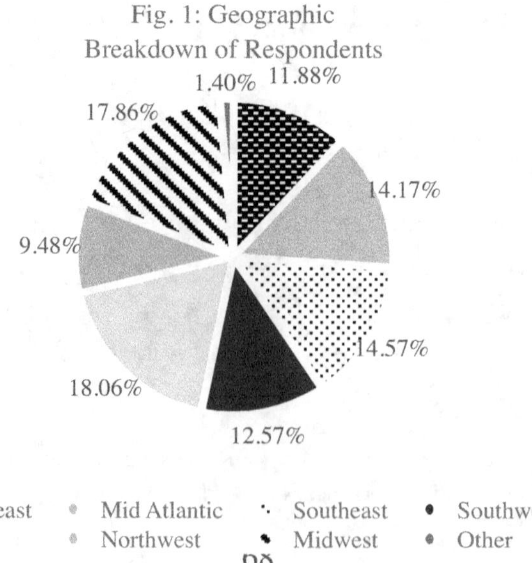

the Northwest, and 18% were from the Midwest. These findings are displayed in Figure 1.

The average age of respondents was 33. We have included a full breakdown of participant ages in Figure 2. Most participants identified as cis females (75%), while approximately 15% identified as cis male, with 3% of participants being trans females, 1% trans males, less than 1% intersex (n=4), and 6% chose other. The sample of participants was also overwhelmingly white (81%) with 9% identifying as Hispanic/Latino, 8% as African American, 4% as Native American, and 4% as Asian.

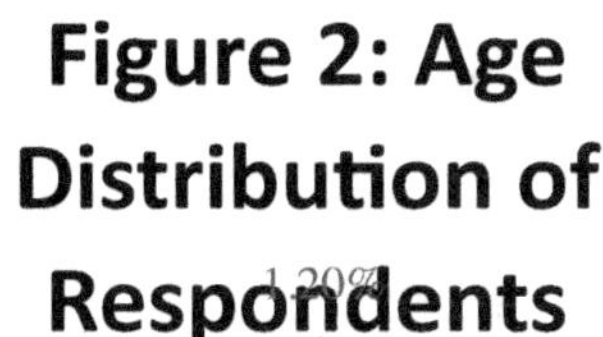

Figure 2: Age Distribution of Respondents

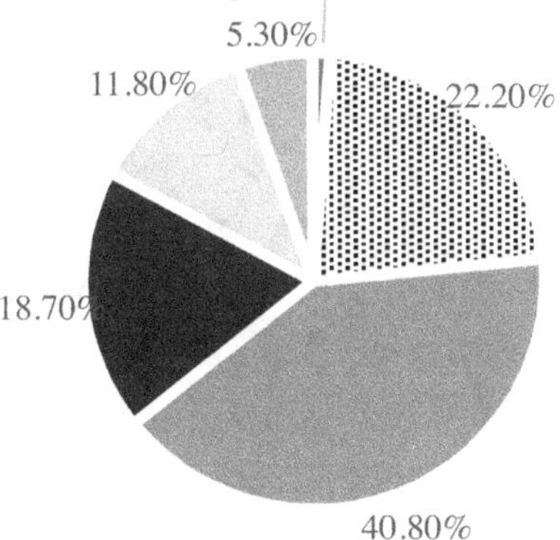

One notable finding is that the majority of participants identified as LGBTQ, with only 37% identifying as straight/heterosexual. This is represented in Figure 3. The participants were highly educated with 92% having finished high school or more, 6% holding a GED, 20% having graduated from a 2-year college, 27% from a four-year college, 10% having vocation/technical training, 11% holding a masters degree, 4% holding a doctoral degree, and 6% having answered that they held some other level of education. While it is possible that there is some sampling bias causing sex workers with more education to have taken this survey, research has found sex workers to be early adopters and innovative users of technology, leading us to believe that the education stats are fairly accurate.

Figure 3: Sexual Identity/Orientation of Respondents

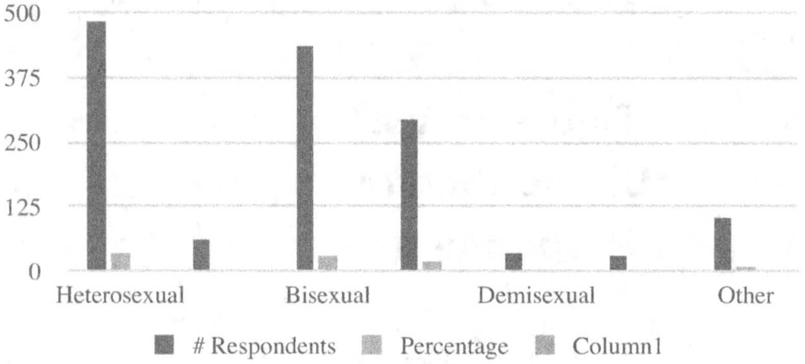

Trans women had slightly lower levels of education throughout, with only 78% having a high school education or more and 18% graduating from a four-year college, 9% having a master's degree, and 5% holding a doctoral degree. People of color respondents had largely the same levels of education as the larger group.

Most participants (87%) reported not having grown up in foster care with 7% answering that they had been in foster care. Most had not been in group homes with only 6% answering that they had. Additionally, 7% of participants had previously served in a juvenile correctional facility. Trans and people of color respondents had higher levels of foster care and juvenile facility involvement - 12% of people of color and 9% of trans people reported being in group homes, 13% of POC and 5% of trans participants reported being in foster care, and 23% of trans women and 10% of people of color reported spending time in a juvenile correctional facility. Most (93%) of participants were US citizens, 4% were legal residents, 2% were undocumented, and 1% chose other.

Conclusion

These survey demographics will help us gain insight into the rest of the data that the survey presents us with. From this data it is clear that the pool of sex workers that we identified is diverse and that no blanket solutions will help solve the problems sex workers face.

Policy Insights

- Programs that aim to help sex workers must be LGBT inclusive.

- Programs for sex workers can expect over half of their participants to be between 25 and 44 years old.

- Sex workers are diverse in every way, there is no one-size-fits-all program.

Chapter 4: US Survey: Family Relationships and Dynamics

Key Findings

- 72% of sex workers are in a relationship, with most relationships being monogamous, and the vast majority are honest about their work with their partners.

- A little less than half of sex workers are able to be honest with their families about their work, with many noting that some family members are aware of their work and it would be inappropriate for other family members (such as children) to know.

- The majority of sex worker parents' children reside with them, have shared custody arrangements, or are adults.

Introduction

This chapter will provide an overview of family relationships and dynamics of sex workers in the United States based on the survey introduced in Chapter 3.

Romantic and Sexual Relationships

Most (72%) of sex workers reported being in romantic or sexual relationships. A majority (58%) of the relationships were monogamous, with 28% reported to be polyamorous and 14% other. The majority of those who checked "other" clarified that they were in a committed marriage that was open to sexual, but not emotional, playtime outside the marriage. Others provided clarification such as: "casual relationships," "asexual," "queerplatonic partnership (we have sex with other people)," "booty call with same person for 5 years," "platonic co-parent," and "mind heart & soul belong 2 only 1 man… but I use my bdy 2 pay bills." These responses reflect not only the diversity of sex worker's relationships, but also the definitions of work, love, and commitment. Most participants did not consider work activities to make them non-monogamous, while two seemingly did.

Do They Know?

Most (80%) of sex workers' partners knew about their sex work, with 14% saying their partners didn't know, and 6% checking "other." Common clarifications of "other" included that their partners were sex workers too, that they only dated casually, that they don't tell people until they need to know, and that their partner knows but doesn't know the extent of it.

Participants were also asked if their self-defined family knew about their sex work. Forty seven percent said that their families did know, while 42% said they didn't know, and 12% said "other." A large majority of the clarifications of "other" were that some family members knew and others didn't. In some cases it was about acceptance – they had told the family members who seemed safe. In other cases it was about appropriateness – adults knew, but not children. Additionally, several reported that it was an open secret or that their family had disowned them because of their work.

Children

Fifty nine percent of participants reported having no children. How does this compare to the rest of the population? It's hard to say. The 2016 census reported that 43% of women under 50 had no children – however our respondents were not only cis women and did include people over fifty. Of those who had children, 42% had one child, 31% had two children, 17% had three children, 4% had four children, 1% had five, and less than 1% six, seven, or eight children; 3% had nine or more children. Children's ages ranged from 6 months to mid-thirties.

Participants were asked whether children were in some form of care or lived with them. Because it was an open-ended question with many "no" answers, several of the answers were unclear. The vast majority of sex worker parents reported that their children reside with them, have a shared custody arrangement, or are adults living independently. Several reported being a primary caregiver of stepchildren. Three reported children in foster care, five with grandparents, one with an aunt, and six respondents placed children for adoption at birth.

A primary predictor of whether a child will end up in foster care is if a parent was in foster care or juvenile detention. Only 13% of sex workers reported being placed in foster care or juvenile detention as youth themselves. Another primary predictor is having a mother in jail – a concern of all sex workers. Although numbers are somewhat unclear about adoption, most adoption agencies report that 20,250, or .5% of children born every year are given up for adoption, while 6 participants (1.7%) reported giving up children for adoption at birth. Heavily criminalized and stigmatized parents face difficult decisions.

Conclusion

Looking at the data on sex workers' family relationships and dynamics gives us insight into the risks that sex workers face when disclosing their status as sex workers. While a majority of the participants noted that their partners were aware of their status as a sex worker, only some noted that they disclose this information to their family members and children. This need to keep one's status as a sex worker private most likely stems from the fear of repercussions from the state: family members reporting them to the police, child services taking their children away, or other means of criminalizing and discriminating against sex work as real work. Looking into the family dynamics of sex workers thus allows us to understand the everyday complications of being involved in the sex industry due to the criminalization of sex work in RI and nationally as well as the general stigma surrounding sex workers as immoral or fallen women. This reminds us again of the difficulty in gathering data about hidden or criminalized populations, and the perceived risk that survey participants endured to provide this data.

Chapter 5: US Survey: Past and Current Labor History

"As a sex worker, I am my own boss. I can make my own schedule and take care of my mental and physical health. I could never do this while working in another sector. I am safer, healthier, and happier doing sex work."

Survey Participant

Key Findings

- 78% of our sample are currently working in the sex industry (sexual or erotic labor).

- The majority of the sample worked indoors, and only 9% were street-based sex workers - but sex workers of color (21%) and trans sex workers (32%) worked on the streets at a higher rate.

- On average, the participants worked in the industry for seven years.

- 73% worked independently with only 9% reporting a coercive circumstance.

- 20% of the sample identified as doing 'survival sex' or sex work in exchange for food, money, shelter or drugs, whereas 12% said they were 'doing sex work to survive' - again, a higher percentage of sex workers of color (27%) and trans sex workers (64%) identified as doing survival sex work.

- 90% have engaged in other types of paid labor, such as hospitality, the food industry, office work, or manual labor jobs.

- Many participants had negative experiences in the formal job market, ranging from typical capitalist country exploitation to discrimination to sexual harassment and assault.

- Participants discussed how work in the sex industry allowed them to set boundaries and protect themselves from the dangers of working in the formal market.

Introduction

This chapter will explore the different types of sex industry work. We investigate some of the reasons that our sample identified for engaging in sex work, such as 'survival sex,' 'doing sex work to survive,' supporting their children, or to maintain control over their work environment. While some participants had favorable responses about work in the formal sector, many discussed exploitation, discrimination, sexual harassment, and sexual assault as reasons why they left formal jobs. For many, sex work allowed them to make a living wage, adequately care for their families, pay for medical bills, and gave them control over their work environments. They had more stability, flexibility, and safety as compared to their experiences in the formal labor sector.

Work in the Sex Industry

Many of our participants did more than one type of work within the sex industry. Indoor work was the most common type of work, with only nine percent engaged in street-based work. Many found clients online. Over half of the sample worked as online escorts (53%), and over one-third found clients through Sugar Daddy websites (35%). Many others worked in the virtual world with nearly half being cam workers (46%) and almost a fifth being phone operators (18%). Other types of indoor work included: working as strippers (33%), masseurs (19%) and doing body rubs/ bodyworks (16%). Twelve percent indicated that they did other types of indoor work, such as working in brothels or as nude/fetish models. Over a quarter worked as dominatrix's (28%), almost a quarter worked as porn performers (24%), and nearly one quarter identified themselves as working within the kinky community (24%).

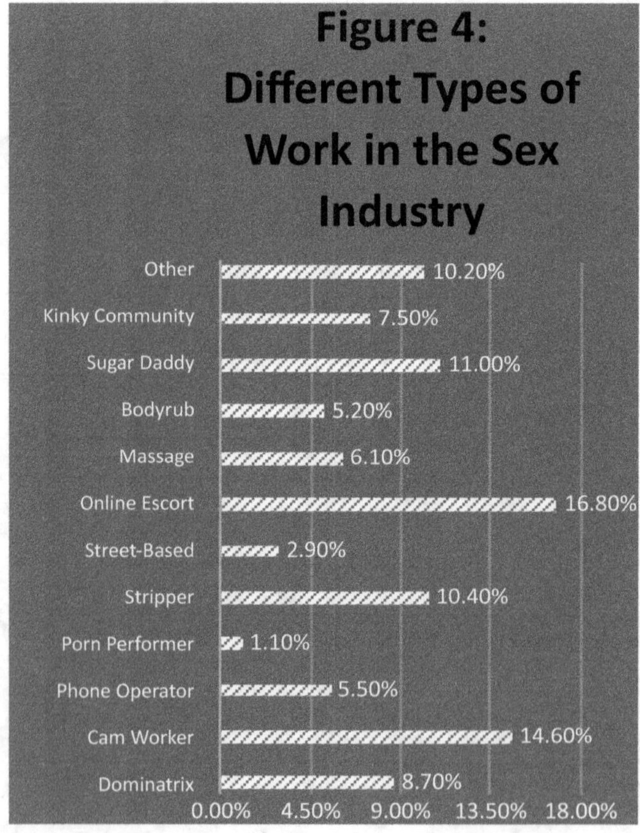

Structural inequalities in society are reflected in the sex industry, with two times as many sex workers of color and over three times as many trans sex workers engaging in street-based sex work. Online webcam work was also less likely to support sex workers of color (35%) and trans sex workers (36%). Trans sex workers were significantly less likely to work as phone sex operators (9%) or strippers (9%). Sex workers of color were more likely to work in massage (30%) or body rubs (28%). Trans women were less likely to be dominatrix's, but more likely (36%) to work in kink.

Who Are They Working With?

The majority of the participants said they worked independently (73%), with sex workers of color working independently a little less frequently (64%), and trans sex workers working independently 77% of the time. Over a fifth worked with someone who was also working in the same way (21%). Almost a fifth of all respondents (16%) said they used sex for survival to access shelter, food, and clothing, but for sex workers of color that number was higher, 27%, and for trans sex workers it was much higher at 64%. Very few participants were in a coercive circumstance (i.e., a pimp, trafficker, spouse, boyfriend, girlfriend, or friend profiting from them (9%).

Survival Sex or Sex Work to Survive?

Historically, 'survival sex' is a term used to describe people who engage in sex work in exchange for money, clothes, shelter, or drugs. It usually refers to runaways or other young people who are homeless and in search of ways to survive or continue to live. The term also applies to adults working in the sex industry who were struggling financially and who are using an exchange system. More broadly, the term includes any sex work in exchange for money, clothes, shelter, or drugs. More categories of sex work are subsumed under this umbrella term.

For some participants, the term resonated with them, especially those who began as homeless teens. One participant said, "Looking back when I would run away from group homes survival sex in exchange for things was something I [did].' After age 19, I started stripping and then online escorting." Another reflected about how they escaped a residential facility and became a homeless runaway. For those who ran away and were living on the street as minors, 'survival sex' seemed an appropriate term.

Participants often had multiple answers about why they participated in survival sex. Almost half who identified as having done survival sex work did it in exchange for shelter (46%). Forty-one percent said it was for food. Over a quarter said it was for drugs (28%) and almost a fifth did it for clothes (19%). Eighteen percent said they did it for other reasons, such as medication, transportation, and even to get a green card.

Other participants had an issue with the term 'survival sex' and 'sex for survival.' One participant said:

> *"Your question about 'survival' requires more clarification. Everyone works to survive. I've worked for major corporations to survive and provide myself with shelter, goods, clothing, and transportation. (-)"*

We agree that it can seem like a meaningless term in the US context where the majority struggle within capitalist structures. Many of us endure jobs that we do not like to pay for the basics, such as rent, groceries, childcare, and others remain in bad marriages for the same reasons. Most of us are struggling to survive, so is most work for survival? Then, is most sex work sex for survival? What delineates 'survival sex,' and 'sex for survival' sex from regular sex work? Another participant said:

"Kind of engaged in survival sex - but, it was something about surviving and between thriving."

The implication in the terms' survival sex' or 'sex for survival' is that one would only do this as a last resort as opposed to 'thriving' or 'making it' and aligning with the United States motto of "pull yourself up by your bootstraps." Some participants identified with doing 'sex for survival' with one participant saying, "I began sex work to afford to survive. Primarily food, after I hadn't eaten in 4 days, I decided it was time." Many participants also engaged in selling sex to survive or where they work in the sex industry to pay their bills, but there is no third party. One participant said:

"I'm not clear on the difference between "acting independently" and "using sex for survival." I was acting independently, but I don't know how else I would have paid for food and shelter, etc. Or is "sex for survival" a direct exchange for food/shelter/etc.? Yeah for me it's always been sex for money to exchange for food/shelter/etc., not a direct exchange."

Based on other participants' comments, these terms can be offensive and potentially triggering. When sex and survival were in the same sentence, participants felt an implication that they were coerced. Some participants felt that they had ownership of their decisions. One participant said, "It was not coercive. I wanted to work, and we all contributed to the household." They did not feel like victims, and it seems that either term 'survival sex' or 'sex work to survive' may signify a victim status. For instance, one participant who said they did 'sex work to survive' demonstrates the necessity of owning their choice:

> *"Did not realize at the time, but it was a last resort. I'm now on disability (severe anxiety & depression) but supplementing the less than $700 a month I get by escorting. Technically, it was survival, but I've preferred not to view it that way, but as more of a choice."*

Is Leaving a Good Idea?

The principal reason participants felt prevented from leaving the sex trade was that they could not make a living wage in the formal market (this was true of 84% of all participants and 94% of trans participants). Thirty-six percent of all participants and 61% of trans participants said that they would be discriminated against because they worked in the sex industry. Ten percent felt they would not get a job because of a criminal record. Only 5% did not leave because someone forced them to stay, 3% said it was because they were minors, and 2% because of their immigration status. Twenty-two percent had other reasons for not feeling able to leave when they wanted.

For some of the female workers, they felt the formal market discriminated against women and that they could retain more control by doing independent sex work. One participant discussed how sex work gave her power which in other circumstances, she did not feel:

> *"I have felt that nobody is going to hire a high school drop-out female that has little skills over a man in the same*

circumstances. Sex work makes me feel like I have control, which is something I don't feel I often have."

For many of the participants, the lack of a basic living wage was overwhelmingly the reason for not feeling able to leave the sex trade. One participant said, "THE ECONOMY. All my other skills literally don't provide enough to cover basics all the time; committing to too many hours at low rates doesn't cover basic bills." Some students who just graduated college were overwhelmed by student debt, and they remained in the industry to pay these loans back. One participant stated: "Student loans are my pimp." Another participant said:

"I live in a city where our rent is 80% higher than the American average. I owe over $100k in student debt, and I'm responsible for my mortgage. I haven't left yet because I'm not stupid. I'd have to earn over $125k a year in my FT job to even consider quitting (the student loans are the true albatross.)"

For some participants, working in the sex industry allowed them to be better parents. In some cases, it allowed them to keep their children; in other cases, it allowed them to pay for insurance, daycare, and after-school activities. One participant said it allowed her to be "like a stay-at-home mom with the salary of someone with an advanced degree." Work in the sex industry allowed them time with their families, and they were able to afford the necessities of life in the United States and provide a good quality of life for their families.

Other participants had life-threatening issues such as not being able to cover required medications. One participant said, "I started two low-paying new jobs and didn't have health insurance yet. I needed life-saving medication. The meds were expensive, and there weren't generics for them yet. It was either sex work or death." Other participants told of how their children suffered from disabilities, and that their children needed care, supervision, or that they could not afford daycare and working, and the sex industry allowed them the time and money to care for their children.

Some of the participants have marginalized statuses, and they feel they could not fit into the formal sector or that they would be rejected by it. These statuses included: being transgender, being disabled, having children with disabilities, having mental health issues, being too young for the licit job sector, having criminal records, and having gaps in employment. Despite many having marginalized statuses, 76% did not collect any benefits (SSI, housing assistance, medical, cash, FS, Social Security) indicating that many qualified people are not getting benefits.

Some participants mentioned that they did not want to hide their work in the sex industry or be stigmatized by work in the formal sector. One participant stated:

> *"I am afraid that employers will discriminate against my work in the sex industry. I want to be transparent, and I am proud of everything I have accomplished. I have skills that would qualify as a good amount of experience in technology fields, marketing, etc. I enjoy the lifestyle and financial comfort that camming has given me. I know I will need to work very hard and finish my college education to be able to obtain a job that pays half as well."*

Many participants said that they never want to leave the industry because of the flexible hours, they enjoy their workmates, they have a steady and sufficient income, and some felt it is thrilling.

Many worked in both the sex industry and the formal market simultaneously. One participant said, "I didn't have any problems leaving-- I always worked a regular job and supplemented with sex work."

Experiences in the Formal Job Sector

Sixty-three percent of participants said around 80-100% of their income was from work in the sex industry. Over a third do other work as a supplemental income or employment in the sex industry as additional income.

Ninety percent of the sample have engaged in work in the formal work sector. The majority of participants' formal economy work experiences were in hospitality (46%), retail (59%), office (46%), and nail salons (7%). Other jobs were labor jobs: domestic workers (16%), construction (6%), agricultural workers (5%), a garment factory worker (2%). Forty-three percent listed "other" as for their work in the formal sector and some jobs listed were in the medical profession, academia, art, and the military.

Exploitation and Degradation

Many participants talked about working long hours for little pay in jobs outside the sex industry, not making a living wage, being paid less than minimum wage, having no sick leave or vacation time, and not receiving adequate medical benefits. One participant discussed how they were exploited, including being verbally and emotionally abused by a boss:

> *"I was extremely exploited. Below minimum wage ($4-5/ hr.) was common.12-hour days were common. At one job, I was not allowed to take water breaks or use the bathroom*

Many of the participants described how formal sector bosses, coworkers, and customers treated them poorly. A number of them discussed how most jobs included exploitation — ranging from those who had high paying corporate or white-collar jobs. One participant reflected on how this is pervasive:

> *"I have consistently been treated like shit at every 'legitimate' job I've ever had. Humiliated, harassed, sexually harassed, transphobia, and underpaid. Corporate America is 100% exploitation, and this is true of all small employers I have worked for as well."*

Many respondents feel that exploitation is part-and-parcel of living in a capitalist country. One participant casually stated, "Exploited (the nature of capitalism), overworked, treated as disposal by upper management/clients, subjected to horrible leadership 99% of the time." Many expected exploitation in the job market, but there was often no return when the regular market job became dangerous for their mental or physical health.

Discrimination

Some employers mistreated those with disabilities. One respondent said, "My disabilities were definitely a problem; I was expected to work and produce quickly, without complaint, and without rest." These respondents were often not provided appropriate accommodations, and they were mistreated and even fired because of their disabilities.

Sexism is every day in the formal work sector, and this is evident based on accounts of masked and openly discriminatory settings. One participant said:

> *"In nearly every industry discussed, women are exploited. We are forced to adhere to weird sexually charged dress codes, whether we're encouraged to show more skin to increase sales or encouraged to be more modest because human bodies are somehow distracting to the workplace environment. We make less than our male counterparts."*

LGBTQIA respondents often identified sexual harassment, homophobia, and transphobia. Employers and coworkers brazenly and subtly discriminated against them at various formal jobs. One participant who identified as a lesbian was fired from her construction job when they found out her sexual orientation. The transgender population is discriminated against, and they have much difficulty in the formal job market. One transgender person said, "Because I am trans - it's hit or miss with jobs - I have been fired for what was probably being trans - after a supervisor left or we were bought by other companies - it always took its toll - Sex work was a fallback." In between being harassed, discriminated against, and fired, some LGBTQIA respondents made money in the sex industry.

Racism was another form of discrimination, and some respondents were openly mocked and abused by coworkers and bosses based on their race. One African-American participant stated, "my hair was made fun of, my facial features were mocked, was often told black women should be pleased to be sexually harassed."

Sexual Harassment

Sexual harassment was familiar with many participants accounting: unwanted comments, advances, touching, and even sexual assault and rape by coworkers, bosses, and employers. These types of work abuse and crimes sometimes started with the participants' first official job. One participant said, "I have been sexually harassed and groped by men I worked for or within jobs I've had outside the sex industry starting at my first job when I was 16." Sometimes these abuses persisted in every work setting. Another participant reflected, "I was degraded and eventually nearly always ended up in a sexual situation in the work environment." Another participant said, "I have been sexually harassed by a previous boss, who even said if I didn't sexually service him, I would lose my job, reputation & credibility in the industry." Minors were particularly vulnerable to this because they had more limited options in the formal sector. One young respondent said, "I was exploited by a manager wanting sex to keep a job as a minor at a Dunkin Donuts."

Some participants who reported sexual harassment or abuse within formal sectors were forced to resign, they were punished or even fired.   A coworker sexually assaulted one participant, and the company punished them. "I was sexually assaulted and harassed by a coworker - when I reported this to my employer, I was suspended from work and only reinstated with a scolding letter putting me on "probation" for "endangering the organization." Another participant who worked as a teacher was forced to resign due to harassment by a supervisor and a coworker who created a 'hostile work environment.

Many participants discussed how they had more control over sexual harassment and abuse when working in the sex industry. A respondent reflected on this "My first day on the job in a nursing facility, I was sexually harassed by a custodian in front of my male peers. I am aware that I feel less able to stand up for myself here than camming or escorting. I think this is because I am working for someone else, and they may not do anything about it." Another discussed having control over harassment and abuse in the sex industry "Office and hospitality work is sexist, I feel much more compromised as a female sexed person in these industries. In sex work, I have more control over how my gender impacts my work life." In many formal work settings, employers ignored, condoned, or even supported sexually harassing or abusive behavior. These experiences made many participants seek work where they had more control over their work environments.

Taking control by managing their work environment felt empowering to many respondents. One participant discussed this change:

> *"I felt more exploited in the restaurant industry than I have so far in sex work, especially camming. My body and sexuality were still a focus and liability at a restaurant, but I wasn't compensated for it. Sex work felt and still feels like capitalizing on the objectification that happens to me in every industry, regardless of the sector."*

Returning or Turning to Sex Work

Based on the survey data, we were able to draw some conclusions regarding the reasons why participants returned or turned to sex work after working in other industries. Of the participants, 78% reported having returned to sex work after spending time working in other industries, but this number was higher for sex workers of color (89%) and trans sex workers (81%). Many respondents preferred to be their bosses, and this allowed many safer and healthier lifestyles. A participant reflected on this "As a sex worker, I am my own boss. I can make my own schedule and take care of my mental and physical health. I could never do this while working in another sector. I am safer, healthier, and happier doing sex work." As previously discussed, the formal sector is dangerous for many people, particularly those who are marginalized. When they decided the rules, work dangers were often minimized.

Participants often discussed how sex work set them free from having to endure mistreatment and abuse in the formal sector. It allowed them freedom. One respondent said, "I did not return to sex work; I TURNED to it." Another participant reflected:

> *"Sex work is liberating. At least for me. I started because I had to survive and pay my way through college. Yes. After less than a year, I started enjoying it. Being my own boss, setting up my own schedule, working when and how much I want, meeting new and interesting people...I wouldn't trade this for anything. Is not only about money. It's about not being a 9 to 5 slave to the system."*

Aside from their negative experiences in the formal sector, many returned because they enjoy the work. One said, "I loved it and missed it." Another discussed how it is better than other options "I both enjoy sex work, and find it intellectually engaging in a way most other jobs aren't." Many participants not only preferred work in the sex industry, but they enjoyed it. One participant discussed some reasons why they prefer this type of work "I get to have fun while I work. I am able to be mentored by and associate with people that are well known high-status professionals, athletes, and politicians that I would never associate with otherwise."

Other respondents felt that work in the sex industry was not only beneficial for them but also their clients. A respondent said, "I enjoy it. It is something I excel at. Moreover, I think it can be used to help people. The extremely socially awkward, the old and lonely, self-improvement. All of these can benefit."

Conclusion

Many of the respondents reported negative experiences working in the formal job sector. These negative experiences (such as discrimination, harassment, not being able to make a living in a capitalist economy, etc.) were often the reasons respondents found themselves doing survival sex or remaining in the sex industry. As long as the formal job sector continues to fail those in it, the sex industry will remain an important means by which people are able to support themselves and their dependents, so it is important that we listen to sex workers and protect their rights, as resorting to or remaining in the sex industry is often the result of the failure of the formal economy to provide for its workers.

Policy Insights

- Programs aimed at helping the 9% of sex workers who reported experiencing coercive work conditions should not expect to serve the other 91% of sex workers.

- Many sex workers reported experiencing harassment and violence in the formal job market and see sex work as an arena where they can set their own boundaries and be free from the hazards of the formal job market. Programs aiming to "rescue" them from sex work and put them back into the formal job market are likely to be rejected.Chapter 6: US Survey: Accessing Public Services

"The hospital staff at the ER were very nice until the police showed up to take my report and once they found out I was an escort they told me that if I wanted to press charges against the man who raped me, that I would be arrested for prostitution. At this point, the hospital staff got cold, distant, and some of them became downright rude to me."

Survey Participant

Key Findings

- An overwhelming majority of sex workers that reported using shelter services also reported that the shelters did not adequately support them.

- 93% of those that reported using social services, reported that they did not disclose their status as sex workers as this made it difficult to obtain support. Sex workers of color and trans sex workers were slightly more likely (12% and 17%) to disclose their sex worker status to service providers.

- The accessibility and quality of legal services sought out by sex workers in the survey appeared to be highly variable but favored legal aid from private attorneys over the public.

- For both accessing medical and mental health services, respondents reported the need for medical professionals to listen to sex workers and educate themselves more on the profession so that they can provide more valuable help.

Introduction

This chapter will explore the accessibility of accessing public services for sex workers, such as shelters, social services, services for those facing prostitution-related charges, legal services, medical services, and mental health services. We will analyze the qualitative and quantitative data provided for by the surveys COYOTE RI put out both nationally and locally in Rhode Island. This chapter will explore the qualitative data and recommendations given directly from sex workers in order to propose reforms, improvements, and ways in which shelters, medical professionals, and other services can better adjust to fit the needs of those involved in the sex industry. In order to effectively serve sex workers and sex trafficking victims, we must listen to them about obstacles to obtaining services and how to improve the accessibility of services.

Accessing Shelter Services

In the U.S., only 12% of respondents (but 37% of trans respondents) noted seeking services from a shelter while in RI only 15% responded that they had sought services from a shelter. Of those that did seek help from shelters, 100% of Rhode Island respondents reported it was a homeless shelter (with 33% reporting they sought out a domestic violence shelter, 17% adult shelter, and 0% youth shelter). Whereas the US survey respondents reported a majority seeking out homeless shelters (47%) with the next most popular shelters being domestic violence (37%) and youth (30%) shelters.

Experiences

Of those that sought out shelters in the US survey, 79% of all respondents, 89% of POC respondents, and 88% of trans women respondents reported that the shelters did not adequately provide them with the resources they needed. Of those that responded yes, they were asked to elaborate and provide examples of resources that they found were helpful, such as counseling, food, clothing, a place to sleep, providing medical care, helping with bills, finding housing, providing a shower, and providing laundry services. One respondent sarcastically noted, "services have demanded to cut off stable 'day jobs' and becoming completely dependent upon their 'salvation' by going completely broke with no income." Although some respondents felt the shelters were able to provide them with helpful services, most reported that this was not the case and, as this respondent notes, oftentimes in order to receive any "salvation" one needed to be able to prove they had no income which acts as a barrier to providing services to everyone who needs them.

Of those that responded "no" to whether or not shelters were able to provide the resources, their explanations largely focused on the lack of resources available (such as only providing insecure sleeping arrangements and food provisions), instances of further abuse occurring (one noted witnessing a woman with a small child being assaulted at a shelter as the reason she stopped going and another noted being assaulted twice while seeking out emergency shelter and that it was easier to sleep on the streets or trade sex for a place to sleep), having to adhere to a narrative of victimization, discrimination (one person noted that the shelter they sought out did not allow transgender people and another simply stated "racist"), not having urgent enough needs, faith-based shelters forcing their ideologies and an overall feeling of discomfort at the shelter. Overall, the concerns of the respondents and the negative experiences they reported regarding their shelter experience reflects the way in which shelters do not adequately provide for those that most need their assistance while in some cases also perpetrating additional harm.

When asked if the shelters were made aware of the respondents' involvement in the sex industry, 85% of Rhode Island respondents answered "no" while 54% of US respondents responded "no" and 9% responded "only certain staff members". This exhibits how sex workers often have to succumb to the social stigma surrounding their work in order to even obtain services from a shelter. Sex workers should not have to keep their profession private in order to obtain necessary life resources.

What Was Helpful/Unhelpful?

Respondents were asked to comment on what aspects of the shelters they had experience with they found helpful, unhelpful, and recommendations they would have for shelters for dealing with people involved in the sex industry. Some of the things people noted were helpful included support groups/counseling, when the staff did not freak out when they revealed their profession, when the staff did not ask too many questions when they offered safe shelter, food, and transportation, and they "gave us a place to be kids". However, most answered something along the lines of "nothing" and a few provided instances in which the shelters perpetuated more harm: "Hmm, gave my abuser access to me, let him order a cab for me to his place", "Threw me back 2 the sharks", and "Literally nothing. Emergency shelters are not even remotely equipped to serve LGBTQ people, nevermind sex workers." Although some of the respondents reported positive experiences, for the most part, the respondents reflected negative and even harmful experiences. Some of the things people noted were not helpful included: being rude/judgmental and not understanding of people's situations, disclosing someone's sexual identity to staff members, allowing guests to be assaulted and/or staff perpetrating abuse, the shelter did not have the resources people needed and/or blatantly denied people resources, embezzlement of donations, gossiping, forcing people to discuss trauma in order to receive resources and sometimes denying them help after they have disclosed traumatic experiences, trying to "reform" sex workers, discrimination, forcing medications, and much more.

Recommendations

Some of the suggestions provided for shelters workers included providing support groups/mental health support services, provide more resources (safe sex resources and contraceptives, health care, employment opportunities, family planning, how to pay rent, etc.), have someone available to assist with filling out paperwork, do not judge or gossip about sex workers or try to reform them, allow people to remain in shelters for indefinite amounts of time even if they are working, do not turn sex workers away ("And don't report minors engaging in survival sex work or tell their parents where they are. So many LGBT kids run away from abusive homes and engage in survival sex work to get by. Let them decide which of those things they would rather do."), harm reduction, and overall foster a safe and inclusive environment. Overwhelmingly answers referred to being non-judgmental, understanding of sex workers, and taking the time to listen to them.

Accessing Social Services

In the US survey, respondents were also asked about whether they accessed social services such as food stamps, welfare, and Medicaid. Of those that responded, 53% (but only 37% of trans respondents) said "yes". Most of those that elaborated noted that they used these services sporadically or during difficult periods of their lives with a few noting that they used these services consistently. Of those that reported using these services, 69% reported that they were helpful, with 11% reporting that they were not, and 20% stating other reasons, with most reasons being that they sometimes helped and in other times did not. Of those that reported having used social services, 93% reported that they did not disclose their status as sex workers.

What Was Helpful/Unhelpful?

Once again, we asked sex workers to explain what was helpful or unhelpful about accessing social services and to give recommendations for social workers. Some of the things that were noted as helpful were assistance with bills and accessing health care. There were a great deal more responses noting things that were unhelpful, including being denied services, being arrested, social workers acting like they were criminals, withholding payments if they are made aware of evidence proving you have an income, only wanting to do the bare minimum to help, and having to go through hoops to get any support. Based off of people's reports of what was helpful versus not helpful, it seems that social services were made difficult to obtain for anyone engaging in sex work as they could not prove their income, were at risk of being arrested or face other consequences if they disclosed, and it was easy for people with social services to deduce that they were sex workers if they reported having no income but were still able to survive. Overall, most people seemed to feel that social workers made sex work a barrier to receiving services even if they were in need of them and largely reported that they did not receive social services while simultaneously engaging in sex work.

Recommendations

Similar to suggestions given for shelter services, respondents largely called on social services to withhold judgment, regard sex work as real work, create a branch of social services dedicated to dealing with those involved in sex work, work from a "trauma-informed model of care", educate workers on harm reduction, allow sex workers to safely disclose their work and/or income, provide free safe sex education services and contraceptives.

When asked if they have ever faced bias, hostility, or refusal of services because of their status as a sex worker, 45% of all respondents, 50% of POC respondents, and 78% of trans respondents reported "yes". When asked to elaborate on their answer, many expressed having been denied services when people became aware of their profession (denied housing, food stamps, etc.) and experiencing harassment (from landlords, co-workers, doctors, social service providers, etc.). Many however expressed that they do not ever disclose their status as sex workers, due to these concerns.

Accessing Court Ordered Services

In the next section of the survey respondents were asked whether or not they had ever been arrested for prostitution or prostitution-related crimes, 84% of the US respondents responded "no", with 16% responding "yes". Of those that responded yes, some noted that they had been referred to trafficking courts, diversion programs, drug courts, or that they had to do community service and were then asked to elaborate on the specificity of the program or service they were asked to do.

Experiences

Of those that elaborated, experiences ranged from being fined, a few reported being referred to a diversion program, some were given probation, many had to complete community service hours, one was made to see a social worker until their lawyer had the charges dismissed, one responded "drug court" while two others responded "trafficking court" and "federal court", one was ordered by the NYC trafficking court to go to yoga and self-esteem courses, one reported having to attend therapy, and some reported being forced into drug or rehabilitation programs against their will even if they were clean. One respondent answered: "They tried to TRAFFICK me into their fucked-up diversion program where I might add the counselors they order you to see are not even licensed to brainwash you into thinking you are doing something wrong or you are a bad person. The only thing bad is the way they Shane people. I'll stay sucking dick over being hungry and you ought to be ashamed of blaming SW for your problems in your marriage I didn't take those vows you did."

Of those that reported participating in these court-ordered services/ programs, about half responded that they had completed these programs while the other half responded "No". Those that answered no provided explanations such as not being willing to pay the money, "fuck diversion", not having the money to pay for bus fares and being sentenced to jail time as a result, or that they fought the charges. Only one of the respondents that completed their program responded in a positive light, "Yes. It was great. The therapeutic setting, no judgment, hooked me up with lots of aftercare including the purple clinic."

What Was Helpful/Unhelpful?

The respondents were then asked if they felt these programs were beneficial to them and were given the capacity to elaborate if they chose to do so. Of those that this question was applicable, only 4 responded yes, another responding "I guess so. I just wanted to finish my probation" and with two others responding that the only part that was helpful was that it allowed for charges to be expunged. The rest of the respondents either replied "no" or gave more critical explanations such as:

> *"No. If anything it put me into it more"*

> *"Of course not. There is nothing wrong with sex work. You think it is not sex workers."*

> *"Not other than showing me how important screening is"*

> *"Really!? Brainwashing is helpful!!!???"*

> *"No, I need help with finding steady income"*

> *"NO, I spend 3 months trying to comply. I was promised help with housing that never happened. They wouldn't even help me with bus fare"*

> *"Not at all. In fact, having to pay 500.00 put me at even more risk of homelessness and drove me into situations that I would not have chosen for myself simply because I wanted to not be homeless"*

"No. They pushed their own agenda on me. I didn't need help."

Not only did respondents express that these programs were not helpful, but in some cases, they perpetrated additional harm and merely served to reaffirm respondents' involvement in the sex industry, the opposite goal of the courts in requiring them to do these programs. These programs neglected to target the real issues that respondents expressed needing assistance with, such as housing. In many cases, the respondents did not feel they needed help and felt that the diversion programs in particular unfairly victimized them for their profession. Based on the respondents' tones and answers, it appears that most felt the court-ordered programs and solutions were not only unhelpful but largely a waste of time and energy for both themselves and the courts. Many respondents were forced into unnecessary programs, such as drug rehabilitation despite not being drug users, or made to attend diversion programs that depicted them as victims when they did not feel that was the case. This uncalled-for victimization is largely due to an ignorance of the sex industry and an outdated standard of ethics regarding sex. If more time, money, and energy was put into understanding sex work as opposed to criminalizing it, the court would be able to target more important issues at play. The overall takeaway from these responses is that the services and programs put in place to "fix" sex workers after facing prostitution-related convictions are generally not helpful and rather conflate issues that are unrelated as being a product of involvement in the sex industry.

Later in the survey, we asked respondents if they had ever completed a diversion program through the courts due to a prostitution conviction and to elaborate on what type (CPS involvement, drugs, domestic violence, family responsibility, etc.).

Although most responded that they had not completed such a program, some did. Their responses included: drug counseling/ rehabilitation, "whore school in Chicago" and other prostitution diversion programs or classes, "I was told to give my DNA, fingerprints and to pay 500.00", a rehabilitation program for at-risk youth, trafficking court, and an AIDs awareness program. Two respondents expressed dealing with religious groups who were trying to stop them from engaging in sex work, with one writing, "Yes, a prostitution diversion program. It was run by Christians and included cops coming in and telling us we'd be raped and murdered and no one would care. It was awful, but it got the charges dropped. I didn't have kids and wasn't using drugs, so nothing about that."

Accessing Legal Services

In terms of accessing legal services to deal with prostitution-related charges, 37% of the US survey respondents reported using a private attorney, 32% reported using a public defender, and 32% reported "other" and were then given the capacity to elaborate if they chose to do so. When asked if the legal aid they received was helpful, 24 of 64 responses (38%) reported yes, 14 (22%) responded no, with other respondents either saying the question was not applicable to their situation or providing an alternative response such as that they had represented themselves in court. Of those that reported their legal aid was not helpful, they gave reasons such as:

> *"No. My private attorney knew I was being trafficked. They showed up intoxicated at one of my court dates and was arrested, and a bench warrant was issued for me, and no one told me until I was arrested two weeks later for the*

outstanding warrant. ... My public defender was utterly clueless about the sex industry and viewed me as another low-life criminal between the DUIs and disorderly conduct cases she had on her workload."

"No, would have preferred someone who specialized and cared about sex works specifically."

"No took my 25.000.00 and plead me out. I was 17 when it happened they charged me as an adult."

"No, they acted in the best interest of the court NOT me"

Based on the survey data, accessing legal aid appears to be more accessible to sex workers than other services, such as shelters and social services. However, the effectiveness and quality of legal aid is highly variable. Of those that chose to elaborate on the question regarding whether or not their attorneys were helpful in finding them not guilty or reducing their prostitution-related charges, only 25 of the respondents explicitly stated the word "yes" in their answer and of those 25, 18 reported having a private attorney with only 8 reporting having a public attorney. Of those respondents that explicitly stated "no" in their answer, about half of the respondents reported having used a public attorney and half private. Given the nature of the small pool of respondents that explicitly stated "yes" or "no" in their responses, it can not be deduced that this data remains true for all sex workers facing prostitution-related charges. However, given the fact that a majority of those that reported their attorneys were helpful also reported having used a private attorney, it is safe to say that the quality of aid received from private attorneys is generally higher than public attorneys in fighting off prostitution charges. It's significant to note that none of the trans participants reported using a private attorney. This correlation is most likely due to the amount of money some respondents were able to provide their private attorneys as opposed to using public attorneys who are a component of the state and ultimately, as many of the respondents expressed, serve the court over their clients.

Accessing Medical Services

In the RI survey, respondents were asked to comment on their experiences seeking medical services. They were asked to elaborate on what was helpful, unhelpful, and what to tell medical providers for how to better serve those in the sex industry. Of those that reported medical services being helpful, they generally said that they did not disclose their status as a sex worker. Medical professions that did not ask too many invasive questions were also reported as being helpful. Additionally, a few respondents noted that Planned Parenthood and checking for STDs were helpful.

Experiences

Many of the respondents expressed that they either never disclose or usually refrain from disclosing their status as a sex worker for fear of judgment. While stigmatizing sex work was the main concern voiced throughout the responses, other respondents shared some more traumatic experiences with medical professionals who failed to help them and, in some scenarios, caused more harm once the respondent's status as a sex worker was disclosed. Some of these instances include:

"When I was working, I was tested for STIs every three months. I used condoms with every client and did not offer anal sex. When I told the nurse at the city clinic that I was a sex worker, while doing a vaginal exam, she stuck a cotton swab in my anus with no

warning. I felt violated. To best serve sex workers, listen to them. If they need additional information, educate them. If I do not perform anal sex, there is no reason to check for STIs in that area."

"The hospital staff at the ER were very nice until the police showed up to take my report and once they found out I was an escort they told me that if I wanted to press charges against the man who raped me, that I would be arrested for prostitution. At this point, the hospital staff got cold distant and some of them became downright rude to me."

These traumatic experiences with medical professionals act as a barrier for sex workers to accessing medical services as the medical professionals that you should be able to trust are the ones perpetrating harm. The majority of the recommendations for medical professionals that respondents provided was to be non-judgmental, provide more easily accessible (and free) STI testing/ clinics, and more low-cost testing and sexual health centers (especially for men).

Mental Health Services

The next question in the RI survey asked the respondents to reflect on any mental health services they had sought out and once again note anything that was helpful or unhelpful and recommendations they have for mental health professionals. Only one respondent had an overall positive comment that did not critique mental health services, "mental health providers were helpful + I knew they had to keep my confidentiality." Most of the comments of those that chose to elaborate reflected negative experiences. Some expressed experiences with mental health professionals shaming them, trying to convert them, and overall not understanding sex work as a profession. Many of the respondents expressed concern over mental health providers shaming and trying to talk sex workers out of their jobs. One explained that:

> *"Within the medical community, the narrative is that sex work is not a choice. Most professionals believe that sex workers are addicts, victims of abuse, or mentally ill. This narrative needs to change. Unfortunately, the only sex workers who come forward are those who need help. Most of the mental health professionals I talked with urged me to leave the industry. One harmed me by telling me I must have been abused and how horrible it must have been that I blocked it out. And oh my god, your mother was an alcoholic. No wonder you are a sex worker. That conversation sent me into a tailspin, feeling really awful about myself."*

One respondent recommended the "tips for mental health professionals" offered by PROS Network-Chicago for a resource for Mental Health providers and mentioned that the only mental health provider they had trusted enough to confide in was one they met at a sexuality-based event. This tendency of mental health providers being untrustworthy, unknowledgeable, or understandable about the sex industry and even perpetrators of harm for sex workers makes accessing necessary mental health help difficult. When medical professionals jump to the conclusion that all of one's mental health issues are related to sex work, that prevents professionals from targeting the real issues at play.

Conclusion

By listening to the voices of the respondents in this survey, it is apparent that accessing public services for sex workers is a major area of concern as a number of barriers exist that often prevent them from seeking and attaining the support they need. Shelter services, social services, court-ordered services, legal services, and medical services are all crucial areas of support that many people need in order to survive. By being judgmental about sex work, not providing the resources that sex workers claim they actually need, not listening to sex workers, and conflating sex work with sex trafficking, the professionals in these fields continue to allow sex workers to fall through the cracks by not providing them with the same support that other individuals receive. In order to improve access to public services, it is vital that professionals are educated on the reality of sex work and do not continue to adhere to dated ethics regarding sex. Amplifying the voices of those in the sex industry is a crucial step in making public services more accessible to sex workers, as they are the people who have had firsthand experiences with the ways in which public services do not adequately support sex workers and know the ways in which the different branches of public services could improve their assistance. Although not all of the anecdotal reports regarding public services reported negative experiences, an overwhelming majority did, which highlights the ways in which public services need to be improved.

Policy Insights

- Increasing the accessibility of emergency shelter and other services can help prevent victimization and other bad experiences in the sex industry.

Chapter 7: US, RI, and AK Surveys: Trafficking, Exploitation, Violence, and Arrests

"I was more scared of the police than of my pimps most of the time."

Survey Participant

Key Findings

- Those who had been victimized within the sex industry reported higher rates of violence from police and were more likely to be turned away, threatened with arrest, or arrested when trying to report a crime they had been the victim or witness of to the police.

- 47% (RI), 52% (US), 74% (AK) of respondents reported being the victim or witness of a crime related to their work that they did not report to police. 59% of (US) respondents of color reported being a victim or witness of a crime they didn't report to police.

- Of those who did try to report to police, police only took reports from 21% (RI), 44% (AK), and 57% (US) and arrested 6% (AK) while they were trying to report.

- 11/1/26% reported being sexually assaulted by a police officer and 15/9/2% reported being robbed by a police officer.

Introduction

This chapter pulls data from the Alaska, Rhode Island, and US surveys to dive into the relationships between sex workers and police that encourage or discourage the reporting of violent crime. Sex workers are important partners in public safety: when Alaska passed a law allowing sex workers and sex trafficking victims to report heinous crimes without being charged with prostitution, sex trafficking cases dropped from 4-5 per year in the two years preceding the change and the year of the change to a total of 1 case with a fictitious victim being pimped out by undercover agents in the two years following. Although reports from sex workers, sex trafficking survivors, and clients are key to fighting trafficking, they are often fearful of arrest or losing their children if they do report. In this chapter, we'll explore the experiences sex workers have had with the police which impact their decision to report violent crimes such as sexual assault or sex trafficking.

This chapter draws data from three surveys: the Alaska survey, the Rhode Island Survey, and the US Survey. Although the three surveys were very similar, they were not identical. The Alaska survey asked participants whether they had ever been a victim of force, fraud, or coercion within the industry or worked as minors (conforming with the federal definition of sex trafficking), while the US survey asked if they had entered the industry under conditions of coercion, and the Rhode Island survey did not ask any variation of this question. Comparing responses of those who've been victimized within the industry to the larger group of sex workers helps us understand how current policy serves the most vulnerable and victimized sex workers.

The chapter ends with policy recommendations, advice for police, and descriptions of experiences reporting crime from participants. Because this research centers the participants – those at the center of the conversation – their responses are included verbatim. Please honor the bravery of the participants who shared difficult experiences by reading all of them – and be aware that there are descriptions of violence and institutional abuse.

Reporting Violence

Forty-seven percent of Rhode Island participants, 52% of US participants, and 74% of Alaskan participants reported being the victim or witness of a crime within the industry that they didn't report, but for marginalized groups that number was much higher: 59% for people of color and 86% for trans people (although only 14 trans people answered this question). The most common reason for not reporting was a belief that the police wouldn't do anything, followed by concern that they or somebody else would be arrested or harassed by police.

In the US survey, those who had been victimized within the sex industry, and might be called trafficking victims, were slightly (4%) more likely to have their reports taken than other sex workers, while in Alaska victims were 14% less likely to have their reports taken by police. In both surveys, those who had been victimized within the industry were more likely to be arrested or threatened with arrest when reporting a crime. Those who had been victimized within the industry were more likely to try to report a crime.

	National (In Person)	National (In Person, Coerced)	Alaska (All)	Alaska (Victims)	Rhode Island (All)	National (All)
Tried to Report	21%	27%	32%	20%	80%	21%
Turned Away	45%	40%	66%	79%	80%	43%
Threatened or Arrested	22%	33%	39%	27%	80%	21%
Didn't Report	56%	76%	74%	47%	50%	52%

One research participant said that when she tried to report a sexual assault, police "made fun of me, called me names and asked me 'what did I expect.' They told me that if I wanted to report a client who raped me that they would arrest me for prostitution." Another participant's advice for police is, "when you see a lady running up to the patrol car that tells you she was attacked, you shouldn't call her a whore and tell her that it is her fault, offer to drive her home and then rape +threaten her." Experiences like this do not lead victims to think of police as people who will protect or pursue justice for them. When sex workers don't report violence because of incidents like these, violent criminals are able to continually prey on marginalized people with impunity.

Other Experiences with Police

Additional factors that go into making a decision to report violent crimes to the police are previous experiences with police. In

Alaska and US surveys, victims within the industry were far more likely to have been robbed, assaulted, or arrested by police officers. In Alaska, those who had been victimized within the industry were over two times more likely to be sexually assaulted by police. Overall, Alaskan sex workers reported the highest rate of sexual assault by police officers (26%), with Rhode Island reporting a little less than half that (11%), and in the US survey, only 2% of escorts reported sexual assault by a police officer. This may be a reflection of overall sexual assault rates: according to the FBI's Uniform Crime Report, Alaska has four times the national average rate of sexual assault. The following chart represents the numbers of participants sexually assaulted, robbed, or arrested by police officers on the different surveys.

	National (In Person)	National (In Person, Coerced)	Alaska (All)	Rhode Island (All)	Alaska (Victims)	National (All)
Sexually Assaulted	2%	2%	26%	11%	60%	1%
Assaulted/ Robbed	2%	5%	9%	15%	50%	2%
Arrested Ever	15%	24%	73%	35%	100%	11%

In the US Survey, 6% of trans sex workers reported being assaulted or robbed by a police officer, three times more frequently than other participants.

One respondent reflected on their experience: "I was raped by a cop that came to visit me and didn't want to pay. He told me that if I said anything that I would be raided and gang-raped by other cops. I know 2 other Providence escorts that have to pay off a cop every week + give him a freebie or he will make sure they go to jail." Another wrote, "The cop told me that if I told anyone that he raped me, other cops would come looking for me, and they would rape + kill me. He took my ID and copied down my name and address and he knows where I live."

Whether sex workers have had an experience like these themselves or have only heard of it happening to a colleague, these sorts of assaults do not inspire sex workers to see police as people they can turn to for help. One sex worker wrote, "I was more scared of the police than of my pimps most of the time." When sex workers do not report rapists and sex traffickers, public safety suffers.

Recommendations for the Police

In the responses to this question, every participant advised police to take reports from sex workers respectfully or investigate crimes against sex workers more seriously. The participants had ideas about how that could be accomplished. Several suggested sensitivity training. Others suggested a police liaison or other unspecified mechanism for sex workers to report crimes. Additionally, several suggested that police become partners in the fight for decriminalization and that in turn police regard sex workers as important partners in the fight against sex trafficking and other violent crime.

Policy Insights

- Sex workers are valuable partners in the fight against sex trafficking and other violent crimes, but the vast majority currently do not report to police when they are victims or witnesses. This can be remedied by decriminalizing sex workers, their support workers such as drivers and bookers, and their clients so that they can report without fear of arrest or losing their businesses. A harm reduction measure would be to create immunity for sex workers and their associates when they are reporting serious crimes such as sex trafficking, child pornography, or kidnapping.

- Public safety could also be greatly improved by a policy requiring police to take reports from sex workers and prohibiting them from arresting or threatening to arrest sex workers who are making reports.

- Policy prohibiting police officers from robbing or sexually assaulting sex workers, and providing for an appropriate response when they do, would increase sex workers' reports and cooperation with criminal investigations.

Chapter 8: US, RI, and AK Surveys: Criminal Laws

"If something bad happens to one of us we are very unlikely to wish to report it as we know we could be arrested or hassled, assaulted, and more. Most criminals know this and count on that fear to be able to victimize us, and quite successfully. That's a huge risk factor for people in this work."

Survey Participant

Key Findings

- State sex trafficking laws vary a lot an in many cases define normal sex work practices like having a place of prostitution (i.e., working out of a hotel room or other indoor location) as sex trafficking.

- Sex workers generally estimate that sex trafficking, according to their own common-sense definitions, occurs rarely, but under broad state trafficking definitions they estimate that it happens most of the time.

- Most participants think that sex trafficking should be defined as forcing someone to engage in prostitution, rather than exploiting someone who is a prostitute.

- To prevent sex trafficking, participants recommend the complete decriminalization of consensual adult prostitution and that measures be taken to improve the relationship between police and sex workers, sex trafficking survivors, and clients.

Introduction

Currently, the laws criminalizing sex workers and the people around them are created by religious groups and by sex worker exclusionary radical feminists who have no experience of the sex industry themselves – and their laws reflect their lack of experience, often flying directly in the face of logic. Pragmatism – and feminism – dictate that sex workers and sex trafficking survivors themselves possess the most information about how to improve their own safety. Like the last chapter, this chapter pulls data from the Alaska, Rhode Island, and US Surveys.

What Laws Exist?

Sex workers are often criminalized by three sets of laws – federal laws, state laws, and city or municipal laws. Federal laws are enforced by the FBI, Federal Marshalls, and, lately, Homeland Security. A person who violates federal law is charged in a federal court by the US Attorneys and can be represented by a Federal Public Defender. State laws are generally enforced by state and city police. A person who violates a state law is generally charged in state court by a District Attorney acting on behalf of the state. They may be represented by a State Public Defender. If a person violates a city or municipal law there is a great deal of variation between states and cities as to how it is handled.

Prostitution itself is not criminalized under federal law. Some say that this is because to do so would violate the federal constitutional rights to privacy, to communicate or gather, and to due process. There is a federal sex trafficking law, 18 U.S. Code § 1591, which makes the following things felonies punishable by 10 years to life:

- Any involvement or facilitation of the prostitution of someone under the age of 18, even if the minor has no pimp and is working of their own volition.

- Force, fraud, or coercion in inducing an act of prostitution or in recruitment, transportation, harboring, or generally facilitating prostitution. For example, fraudulently inducing an experienced sex worker to travel to your state to engage in prostitution by lying to them about the fees your agency will charge is the same degree of crime as forcing someone into prostitution with violence or threats against their children.

- Patronizing or agreeing to patronize a minor in prostitution is also sex trafficking. The vast majority of these cases are against men who agree online to pay for sex with a fictitious minor or minors being pimped out by the FBI. This can be quite confusing to the public when they see a headline that a local man has been charged with sex trafficking, but no actual minors were involved and no one except for the FBI tried to pimp out a child.

Additionally, we have a non-criminal definition of sex trafficking under the Violence Against Women Act:

- A person who has been a victim of force, fraud, or coercion in prostitution, worked as a prostitute while they were a minor or a minor who is not engaged in commercial sex but engages in sex acts and receives something of value.

Broadly speaking, most states have had a set of laws dating back to the 1930s against "Promoting Prostitution" aimed at criminalizing pimps. These laws typically criminalized things like having a place of prostitution or driving a prostitute as misdemeanors, though some states included more serious crimes as felonies. Over the last two decades, some states have simply tweaked their promoting prostitution laws and renamed them "Sex Trafficking," turning misdemeanors into felonies, while others have added sex trafficking laws alongside their promoting prostitution laws. Generally speaking, sex trafficking and promoting prostitution laws can both be felonies or misdemeanors and apply to:

- Having a place of prostitution.

- Transporting a prostitute.

- Receiving money from a prostitute.

- Finding a customer for a prostitute or a prostitute for a customer.

- Advertising for prostitution.

- Aiding or facilitating prostitution, such as providing condoms.

- Inducing someone into prostitution.

- Inducing someone into prostitution with force, fraud, or coercion.

- Inducing a minor into prostitution.

- Organizing for prostitution.

Sex workers have complained that these laws are unfairly applied to sex workers themselves (having a place of their own prostitution), their adult children (receiving money from a prostitute), their landlords, contractors they hire for security, driving, or booking, and particularly other sex workers when they work together for safety.

State and city or municipal prostitution laws are often sexist and archaic, applying only to women or with names such as "Being an Inmate of a Place of Prostitution." In Pennsylvania, a sex worker can both be charged with "Having a Place of [their own] Prostitution," and "Being an Inmate of a House of Prostitution" at the same time. In other jurisdictions, constitutional challenges or common sense have caused the laws to be reworded, focusing on an act of commercial sex. Many states and cities or municipalities also have laws against "Manifesting Prostitution," or "Loitering for the Purpose of Prostitution," commonly called walking while trans or walking while black laws. In some jurisdictions, these laws have been found unconstitutional.

What Laws Should Exist?

- What should the definition of sex trafficking be?

- What are the most common risks to people in the sex industry?

- What are the most effective laws to prevent violence against sex workers?

- What are the most effective laws to prevent exploitation within the sex industry?

- What are the most effective laws to prevent sex trafficking?

- What are the most effective laws to protect and promote public safety?

- What is effective or damaging about current laws?

These are all slightly different questions with different answers that we will explore in this chapter. This chapter includes all participants from the RI and Alaska Surveys and participants from the US Survey who had engaged in in-person full-service sex work or full body sensual massages.

Sex Trafficking: Estimating the Scope

How frequently sex trafficking occurs is dependent on the definition of trafficking one uses. Some estimates have tried to count every sex worker in the country as trafficked, while others include youth who are not involved in the commercial sex industry, etc. But wouldn't sex workers be in the best position to know?

Sex workers were asked, "according to your own definition, how often do you think sex trafficking happens in your state?"

Rhode Island:

- 52% think that trafficking happens rarely (2 on a scale of 1-6)

- 36% think that it happens sometimes (3)

- 5% think it happens never (1)

US Survey, only criminalized in-person workers:

- 71% think it happens sometimes (2 on a scale of 1-5)

- 13% think it happens a lot of the time (4)

- 4-6% each thinks that it happens never, about half the time, or always.

Alaska:

- 50% think it happens sometimes (2 on a scale of 1-5)

- 20% think it happens never (1)

- 15% think it happens about half of the time (3)

- 10% think it happens a lot of the time (4) and 5% think it happens all of the time (5)

What if the respondents had been victims of force, fraud, or coercion within the sex industry?

US Survey, victims of coercion:

- 38% think it happens sometimes (2 on a scale of 1-5)

- 35% think it happens a lot of the time (4)

- 10% think it happens about half of the time (3)

- 15% think it happens all the time (5)

Alaskan victims of force, fraud, or coercion:

- 60% think it happens sometimes (2 on a scale of 1-5)

- 20% think it happens never (1)

- 20% think it happens a lot of the time (4)

Do people who've been victims of force, fraud, or coercion within the sex industry consider themselves to be sex trafficking victims?

US Survey:

- 61% yes

Alaska Survey:

- 100% no

The difference in responses may be attributable to the years that passed between surveys.

Now, what if we use legal definitions to try to estimate the scope of sex trafficking? Sex workers were asked, "according to your state laws, how often do you think sex trafficking happens?"

Rhode Island:

- 52% rarely (2 on a scale of 1-6)

- 30% sometimes (3 on a scale of 1-6)

This is only slightly different from Rhode Island sex workers' estimation of the scope of sex trafficking according to their own definitions.

US Survey:

- 41% think it happens all of the time (5 on a scale of 1-5)

- 40% think it happens a lot of the time (4)

- 7% each think it happens about half of the time or sometimes (2-3)

This substantial difference in sex workers' estimation of the scope of sex trafficking under state laws as compared to by their own definitions reflects the broadness of sex trafficking laws.

Alaska:

- 40% think it happens most of the time (4 on a scale of 1-5)

- 35% think it happens all of the time (5)

This is a substantial difference from Alaskan sex workers' estimations of the scope of sex trafficking according to their own definitions, illustrating the broadness of Alaska's sex trafficking law at the time (2014).

Participants Definitions of Sex Trafficking

The large majority of participants in all surveys thought that sex trafficking is, or should be, forced sex work, with an emphasis on a person being forced into sex work rather than a sex worker being coerced to do more or different work than they agree to. A few mentioned that a trafficker takes "all the money." A few discussed movement – that trafficking involves moving someone or limiting their movements. In the US Survey, several people used the terms force, fraud, and coercion, showing that they are familiar with federal law.

Several participants discussed the variability of choice and circumstance that sex workers experience. One said:

"Bullshit. Yes [sex trafficking] exists but a lot of things that get lumped in as "trafficking" are more like domestic violence than organized crime, which I think the term "sex trafficking" kind of implies, something organized. I don't think a husband or boyfriend who pressures a woman to strip or escort or even work on the street is a trafficker. I think he's an abuser, emotional and sexual abuse at least if not physical, but I think "trafficking" implies an organized criminal network in most people's minds and anti-trafficking groups and public figures take advantage of that perception to make the issue sound more "important". I think people are exploited by many industries. If I were undocumented I think I would rather work in a massage parlor than wash dishes or clean hotel rooms. People have options most of the time, it's just that sometimes ALL your options suck. No one "rescues" maids or nannies or nail salon workers. Too many people today think no one should ever have to be uncomfortable or feel exploited for any reason and that is just not realistic. Graduate students are exploited by professors and no one tries to say they are "trapped" in school by debt or whatever. No one denies they have agency. Almost all sex workers have a choice, if you're turning tricks for crack you could stop smoking crack if you hate turning tricks that much. You can go to a shelter or rehab or whatever but they take away a lot of your choices. Sometimes all your choices suck, but that just means life sucks, it doesn't make you any more of a victim than anyone else with a shitty life."

Another participant also discussed boyfriends, saying that sex trafficking is "People forced or sold into the sex industry, or girls who have a boyfriend who will not work and she supports him by the fruits of her labor." A small number of participants shared firsthand experiences of trafficking or definitions that seemed to reflect personal experience:

> *"I was exploited by my pimp and had to do everything he said, he talked to the clients pretending to be me and sent me to various hotels and would collect half. Sometimes I was with a coworker."*

> *"Personally? Being forced or sold into the sex industry. To be mentally brainwashed into believing it was your own choice. To be made to engage in behavior that you wouldn't do on your own accord, while someone else profits off of you. However different states have different laws. In MA, you can be arrested for sex trafficking for owning or even working as support staff for an agency."*

> *"Violent forced. I believe the pump/hoe culture can be positive."*

> *"Also in situations with pimps that use coercion where they make promises they never come through it and when the girl wants to leave they start getting abusive.. or they hook the girl on drugs. Anyone who takes 100% of the profits of somebody else selling their body. I do not feel brothels or agencies who take a percentage with the entertainers' consent as trafficking."*

> *"The forcing or coercion into sex acts by one human being with more power upon another human being with less. This does not include the mutual exchange of money for sex acts, *perhaps* unless the person is a minor- I have mixed feelings on that. I sought out sex work as a minor, but that*

doesn't mean the man should've hired me, and I was given no choice when he wanted to have sex with me."

What Could Be Done to Prevent Force, Fraud, and Coercion Within the Sex Industry?

The majority of participants' answers were evenly split between discussing decriminalizing prostitution so that sex workers can access equal protections of criminal and labor laws, and reducing vulnerability through better social services, economic opportunities, and empowerment for children. One RI participant seemed to sum up many of the responses when they wrote, "better economic and educational opportunities for women, elimination of child abuse, an easier way to report abuse without the worry of retaliation, and raising women to be more secure and men to be more respectful." A US Survey participant wrote:

> *"If they decriminalized prostitution or offered more protection women who were being forced would feel more comfortable asking for help from law enforcement. A lot of women end up wanting to do sex work just not for the person who is exploiting them. That was the case for me once I got away from my pimp I saw the potential for money and that I could keep it for myself and work independently. But in a lot of cases, they won't offer you services unless you stop being a sex worker and conform to all their requirements."*

Of those who discussed making prostitution legal, some thought that it would increase their ability to keep themselves safe from sex traffickers. One US survey participant wrote, "making prostitution legal and allowing people to use means to make yourself safe (drivers, bouncers, a fee to a house that provides all of that)."

Others discussed how being decriminalized would allow sex workers to assist in ending sex trafficking, for example, one US Survey participant wrote, "Decriminalization. I know which pimps are not doing right by their hoes and take advantage. Some hoes benefit greatly from the relationship. If it wasn't so illegal the bad seeds could be singled out instead of everyone being looked at even if the relationship isn't much different than a marriage."

What Could Be Done to Prevent Minors From Entering the Sex Industry?

Participants think we need more and better sex education and education about healthy relationships and work for children. They also wrote that we need a better safety net, particularly housing and economic opportunities, and particularly for homeless and LGBTQ youth. For example, one RI participant wrote, "Change work laws to make room for youth to work without exploitation; support victims of sexual abuse in the home; be vigilant of violence in shelters, group homes, and foster care; support LGBT youth. Most minors who leave home are escaping violence and need money or shelter," while another wrote simply, "Give them resources so they don't have to suck dick."

Again, many wrote about decriminalization, writing things like, "Maybe if the older escorts and clients could report tips on teens without putting themselves at risk for arrest that might help." Another suggested that "Police need to foster relationships with people in the industry that do things right so abuse of children is reported."

One participant shared her personal experience, writing "being a minor who was doing sex work I wouldn't have entered the industry if I wasn't kicked out of my house at 15 yrs old for being a trans woman."

What Are the Real Risks to People in the Sex Industry That Law Enforcement Should Be Concerned About?

Most participants wrote about sexual assault and other violence by perpetrators posing as clients, who know that sex worker are not able to report them to the police without risking arrest themselves. For example, one said, "If something bad happens to one of us we are very unlikely to wish to report it as we know we could be arrested or hassled, assaulted, and more. Most criminals know this and count on that fear to be able to victimize us, and quite successfully. That's a huge risk factor for people in this work."

Many also mentioned "Corrupt cops, unsympathetic cops," and "bad cops wanting freebies, cops who lie, cops who steal." Another participant wrote, "Cops are the primary danger faced by sex workers. They abuse sex workers without consequence due to unrestricted power over them."

Some wrote about stigma and misogyny. One US Participant wrote, "Being assaulted and/or raped while working is number one. Being outed by neighbors, landlords, ex-partners is a risk too or being blackmailed by them. These are the things I was most afraid of when I worked."

Some wrote about other risks imposed by laws, for example: "My friend doesn't want to drive me for legality so I have to take a risk going by myself. Tell that to law enforcement. Laws are STUPID to make it legal! End the bullshit!"

One RI participant mentioned pimps, and two US Survey participants wrote about domestic violence, consistent with Alaskan participants who discussed "boyfriend pimps" who trick their girlfriends into sex work or trick sex workers into dating them and then become violent and/or exploitive. Other than this, no participants mentioned pimps.

What Laws Would Protect People in the Sex Industry?

There was broad conformity in the answers to this question: participants want to be decriminalized so that they can access the equal protections of criminal and labor laws. "Maybe a law that lets you report rape no matter your occupation."

Participants additionally mentioned: age limits, anti-discrimination laws, laws against police having sexual contact with them, making crimes against sex workers hate crimes, laws against "stealth" condom removal during sex, safety zones for street-based sex work, laws criminalizing police sexual contact or penetration with those they're investigating, and enhanced sentencing for violent criminals who target people in the sex industry.

Conclusion

Prostitution, promoting prostitution, pandering, and sex trafficking laws broadly are out of touch with the realities of sex work and make conditions more dangerous for sex workers. Much work is needed to create prostitution policy that makes sense and eliminates sex trafficking and other violence against people in the sex industry.

Policy Insights

- There are large discrepancies between sex workers own definitions and understandings of sex trafficking and some states' legal definitions of sex trafficking. The federal criminal definition is closer to sex workers' perceptions of sex trafficking.

- Sex workers believe that those most at risk of being sex trafficked are women and children who would also be considered vulnerable outside of the sex industry: the homeless, mentally ill, abused, migrants, trans people, and runaways. Programs aimed at reducing the vulnerability of these groups may reduce trafficking.

- The number one way to prevent sex trafficking is to decriminalize all aspects of consensual adult prostitution so that sex workers and our clients, drivers, and others can report trafficking and access the equal protections of the justice system.

- Aside from decriminalization, many youth can be prevented from entering the sex industry by improving their access to housing, employment, education, and social services.

- Police should be concerned about violent criminals who pose as clients to target sex workers because they know sex workers will not go to police, and about people who are forced into prostitution rather than policing moral crimes.

Chapter 9: After FOSTA

"[FOSTA/SESTA] changed the power dynamic for my clients. They know business is hurting…."

Survey Participant

Key Findings

After FOSTA/SESTA and the seizure of Backpage.com, there was an immediate increase in:

- Risk-taking by sex workers.

- Contact from pimps and other predators.

- Demands for cheaper services.

There was an immediate decrease in:

- Income for sex workers.

- Client contacts and inquiries.

- Workers screening clients for safety.

- Workers' bargaining power.

What is FOSTA?

The Stop Enabling Sex Traffickers Act (commonly known as FOSTA or FOSTA/SESTA) became federal law on April 11, 2018. The bill made it criminal sex trafficking for a website to "facilitate prostitution" online, effectively removing all US-hosted advertising websites for sex workers. The passage of FOSTA is commonly confused with the federal seizure of Backpage.com, the biggest advertising site in the world for sex workers. However, Backpage was seized as part of a criminal investigation days before the passage of FOSTA/SESTA.

Imagine that you woke up one morning, drove to work, and the building had simply vanished. That is, essentially, what happened to many sex workers on April 12, 2018. In the aftermath, COYOTE RI developed a survey to track the effects of FOSTA/SESTA on sex workers across the United States. However, it's important to note that FOSTA and the seizure of Backpage also impacted sex workers in other countries – for example, many sex workers in Australia, where sex work is decriminalized, reported losing their income when Backpage came down.

The Research

Coyote-RI surveyed 275 US sex workers in April, May, and June of 2018. The purpose of the survey was to assess the immediate impacts of FOSTA/SESTA and the seizure of Backpage.com on people in the sex trades.

Sex Worker as Breadwinner

Seventy percent of survey participants cited sex work as their sole income before FOSTA/SESTA and the seizure of Backpage.com. Eighty percent were the sole providers for their families. Of those 36% were supporting only themselves, 26% were supporting 2 people, 13% were supporting 3 people, and the remaining 25% were supporting more than 3 people.

More than half (55%) of participants said that their income dropped immediately after Backpage.com was seized, while 10% didn't see a drop in their income for 1-2 weeks and 3% saw no drop for 2-4 weeks. A little over a quarter (27%) saw no decrease in their income at all. One of these people noted that they advertised on Eros, an expensive advertising site used by "elite" escorts, and her income had increased with the closure of Backpage.com.

A little under a quarter (21%) of participants said that they were unable to support themselves and their dependents within less than a week of Backpage being seized, while 15% were unable to support themselves and their dependents within two weeks and 6% within a month. Slightly less than half (49%) were still able to support themselves and their dependents.

Seven percent had been evicted by the time they took the survey, while others commented, "I probably will be [evicted] this month," "not yet, but I will be next week," "will be in May," "No, but my gas is shut off and I'm cleaning myself with hot water from my coffee maker," and "Not yet but I don't have any way to pay future housing costs starting for May."

Risky Work Conditions

More than half (61%) reported having taken riskier, less reputable clients since Backpage.com was seized, while only 33% said they hadn't. Of the people who checked "other," some reported that they were not taking new clients at all. One commented, "I have had an increase in pimps contacting me and known manipulative clients but I refuse to take them. My landlord knows my profession and the consequences of this bill and has offered to commute any loss of income until the market stabilizes."

Thirteen percent of participants reported that they had been a victim of violence since FOSTA/SESTA passed and Backpage.com was seized. Of the 3% who checked the "Other" box for this question, comments ranged from, "a client threatened me with a knife" and "Encouraged to engage in activities outside my comfort zone because I need the income," to "No clients."

More than half (66%) of participants reported that someone had tried to threaten, exploit, or get freebies from them since FOSTA/SESTA passed. Thirty-two percent reported that this had not happened to them, and two percent checked "Other".

Before FOSTA/SESTA passed 92% of participants reported that they screened their clients, while only 63% did afterwards. Screening is the practice of checking a client out by speaking to his references, verifying his employment, checking his criminal background, or having a conversation with him. Sex workers have slightly different screening practices to keep themselves safe. Of those who checked the "Other" box, some comments were, "I still screen them but I see guys now I wouldn't have before. The other day I saw a guy with two assault charges on his record which I never would have done before," "I try to, but have moved to "dating" sites that are in denial about sex work. It's much, much harder to screen since so many sex worker sites went down," "Just working out of clubs. Can't really screen," "it's harder to get clients to cooperate with screening," and "Not nearly as much… when ur desperate u make exceptions."

Sixty percent of participants said more clients than normal were trying to convince them to lower their rates.

Three percent reported becoming victims of sex trafficking since FOSTA/SESTA, with the 2% who checked "Other" leaving comments like, "Coercion, yes. I felt forced to offer discounts to a client in order for him to refer friends," "Threatened by a pimp to work for him," and "Men calling themselves gorilla pimps have been trying to access all the girls since this passed." Since FOSTA/SESTA passed, 33% of participants reported becoming victims of exploitation that they would not consider to be sex trafficking, and 5% reported that a police officer had exploited them for free sex.

Thirty of the participants had specific incidents of violence to report. Their descriptions are chilling. One said,

> *"I am currently held captive financially and legally. I routinely am raped and I have to pretend I enjoy it or suffer emotional violence and threats of physical violence. I am trying to plan and implement an emergency relocation from TX to NY. But I am almost constantly watched and have no way to acquire traveling expenses."*

Another explained, "I live in Miami Fl, I was raped by a client and two of her friends after we had sex, she paid me and then her two male friends showed up and made me fuck them for free." Another participant reported:

> *"Since FOSTA passed I've been working mostly with regular clients, but I can't make my living off of just regulars and it's hard to screen now. So I met with a new client that I had only met that night. I got in his car and we went to his place a town over from where I live. We got to his place and there were four other men there. I was terrified but I was afraid to try to leave because I knew they would probably follow me. I knew I would get hurt if I*

stayed and I would get hurt if I tried to leave. I was gang raped that night by five men. I was not paid. They stole everything I hadn't on me (which was not much.) I was covered in bruises and scrapes and cuts. I did not go to the hospital because I was afraid. I did not tell anyone (except for fellow sex workers so they know not to go with him) because I was afraid."

While another explained:

"This law changed the power dynamic for my clients. They know business is hurting, because I asked for an advance to pay my tuition. My health insurance is a part of that. The first day after Backpage shut down, a client told me I was going to have to start giving him a 2 for 1 deal (free sex every other time) in order for him to get me more clients. I balked at first, but realized I didn't have a choice. I know if he refers people, they are more likely to not be violent and not have STDs, because he has an interest in keeping me safe for his own pleasure, but now I have to have sex for free every other time for him. I urged him not to tell anyone and he told me he should get a better discount for keeping a secret. I live in Chicago. I've been here for only 5 months."

Another participant said a pimp was "exploiting me and trying to 'pimp me out' and 'own me' so I could continue to keep my appartment."

Conclusion

FOSTA/SESTA caused an immediate and dramatic increase in violence, including sex trafficking, against sex workers. The immediate drop in income left sex workers scrambling to meet their and their dependents immediate survival needs, which increased their vulnerability to pimps and other bad actors who sought to assault them, coerce them into unwanted sexual activities, or underpay them. It is essential that FOSTA/SESTA be repealed to prevent sex trafficking and other violence against sex workers.

Policy Insights

- Repeal FOSTA/SESTA.

- Policy makers should listen to sex workers before making laws that will affect us.

Chapter 10: Four Years of FOSTA/ SESTA

About the Survey

In July 2022, COYOTE worked with a small focus group of sex workers and sex trafficking survivors to develop a survey of sex workers and sex trafficking survivors to assess the effects of four years of the Fight Online Sex Trafficking Act, commonly known as FOSTA or FOSTA/SESTA. FOSTA modified the Communications Decency Act to allow for prosecution of website owners whose websites contained user generated content that facilitates or aids prostitution, resulting in an immediate widespread loss of advertising and screening resources.

This survey is meant as an updated follow up to the survey that we did immediately after FOSTA went into effect in 2018. The questions were beta tested on a small sample before being distributed. The survey opened on July 11, 2022 and closed on August 21, 2022. COYOTE RI solicited survey participants by posting on social media and emailing and tweeting escorts who advertise online. In the last few days, participants from groups who were under-represented among survey participants (male workers) were offered $10 to complete the survey. Participants were limited to those who had worked before and after FOSTA's enactment, as verified by a qualifying question. 332 people started the survey and 227 completed it. All responses of all qualified participants are included. Survey questions focused on three areas: FOSTA's effect on violence, FOSTA's effect on vulnerability, and FOSTA's effects on public safety more broadly.

Why the Survey?

We believe that the people most impacted by FOSTA have the most insight into its impacts. As a criminalized population, our voices have always been hidden in the shadows. Legislators do not consult us when they make laws that dramatically change our working conditions, and most of us do not choose to risk arrest by reaching out to them, instead choosing to share our experiences and insights anonymously online. One of the primary effects of FOSTA has been to shut down our online speech and make us even more afraid to speak up publicly. This survey is intended to bring the voices of our community, which sociologists call a "hidden population," to our broader community and to the legislative and judicial communities which are empowered to create the safety and fairness of our work conditions by making and changing laws.

Sex Trafficking: A Note About Language

"Sex trafficking" is a phrase with so many different legal and popular definitions that it has become devoid of any specific meaning. In this report we use the federal definition of sex trafficking: force, fraud, coercion, or minors. Under federal law, minors in the sex industry are victims of sex trafficking even if they are working on their own with no trafficker. For this survey, we split the two groups up - victims of force, fraud, or coercion, and those who entered the industry as minors. There is some overlap between the two groups.

It's important to note that the majority of these people would not call themselves sex trafficking survivors and many would be offended by being called sex trafficking survivors. However, when we discuss federal laws like FOSTA in relation to sex trafficking survivors, these are the people we are talking about. Throughout this report, we have attempted to respect people's rights to self-definition by using the terms "survivors of force, fraud, or coercion within the industry" or "those who entered the industry as minors," while also being clear that these are the "sex trafficking victims" that FOSTA was supposed to help.

Summary

Broadly speaking, FOSTA increased force, fraud, and coercion against sex workers from other actors within the sex trade, and violence from clients and perpetrators posing as clients. At the same time, FOSTA created more vulnerability to violence by reducing income, increasing homelessness, decreasing peer support, and decreasing access to safety information. FOSTA negatively impacted public safety by pushing advertising sites overseas where police are less able to subpoena information from them and by making sex workers and sex trafficking survivors much less likely to report serious crimes, like assault or child pornography, to police. In other words, the real-world effects of FOSTA are completely contrary to its stated intent.

The table below gives responses for all participants, as well as for several subgroups: survivors of force, fraud, or coercion, those who entered the industry as minors, people with disabilities, men, and people of color. Because some participants only completed part of the survey or skipped questions, the number of participants in each group is included for each section of the survey.

Question	All	Trafficking survivor: force, fraud, coercion	Trafficking survivor: entered industry as minors	People with Disabilities	Men	People of Color
TRAFFICKING N=	248-215	56-48	26-25	90-79	17-16	69-60
Reported an increase in force or coercion	40%	**64%**	56%	51%	29%	43%
Reported an increase in fraud	37%	58%	48%	54%	38%	43%
Reported an increase in recruitment by pimps (not trafficking)	55%	56%	56%	46%	**13%**	43%
DANGEROUS EXPLOITATIVE WORK CONDITIONS						
N=		245-238	56-55	88-86	16-15	67-64
Reported an increase in violence from clients or those posing as clients, including stealth condom removal	39%	**67%**	52%	53%	**13%**	34%
Reported increased pressure to provide services outside of their boundaries	54%	66%	68%	67%	31%	59%
Lowered rates	35%	**44%**	31%	**46%**	25%	33%
Offered new services that they weren't comfortable with	41%	**47%**	42%	**52%**	31%	43%

INCREASED VULNERABILITY - WORK CONDITIONS						
N=	53-52	228-221	26-24	87-78	15	65-63
Turned to street-based work	11%	17%	**24%**	21%	**0%**	12%
Did not use blacklists before FOSTA	20%	13%	8%	17%	67%	25%
Did not use blacklists right after FOSTA	39%	**44%**	29%	38%	73%	47%
Currently aren't able to access blacklists	30%	28%	28%	25%	80%	36%
Used 2+ blacklists before FOSTA	68%	72%	84%	72%	27%	
Used 2+ blacklists right after FOSTA	39%	37%	38%	37%	13%	
Use 2+ blacklists now	43%	45%	36%	49%	7%	
Report that FOSTA prevented them from using screening measures that make them feel safe	78%	**81%**	79%	79%	80%	77%
Reluctant or unable to express themselves online in a way that attracts customers who want the services they provide because of FOSTA	75%	77%	**91%**	79%	53%	78%
Reluctant or unable to express themselves online in a way that would prevent customers they don't want from contacting them because of FOSTA	50%	62%	65%	50%	13%	51%
Reluctant or unable to express themselves online in a way that affects their safety because of FOSTA	43%	62%	65%	59%	27%	46%
Reluctant or unable to express opinions online because of FOSTA	60%	63%	70%	60%	33%	52%

INCREASED VULNERABILITY - INCOME					
N = 53-49	227-220	25-23	81-78	15	64-61
Received new public assistance	31%	33%	26%	**44%**	33%	39%
Applied for public assistance, did not receive	17%	20%	26%	22%	20%	23%
Able to be only somewhat financially secure with FOSTA in place	42%	42%	32%	38%	33%	35%
Not able to be financially secure with FOSTA in place	40%	44%	52%	51%	20%	48%
Income dropped	82%	81%	80%	86%	67%	81%
PUBLIC SAFETY					
N=	225-221	52-51	24-22	80-79	15-14	64-61
Less likely to go to police if assaulted now	70%	63%	**78%**	67%	52%	63%
Less likely to go to police if client brought child porn	50%	57%	**77%**	54%	14%	48%
Reported a crime and FOSTA affected investigation	3%	4%	4%	3%	7%	**8%***

this is 100% of the POC who reported crimes to police - for other groups about half of their reports weren't affected by FOSTA

FOSTA Increased Violence and Trafficking Within the Sex Industry

Although FOSTA was intended to decrease sex trafficking it did just the opposite. Results show that 40% of participants reported an increase in force and coercion and 45% reported increased recruitment by pimps after FOSTA. For participants who had been or were currently victims of trafficking, the numbers were 64 and 56% respectively. 36% of participants said that there was an increase in fraud (trickery or lies used to change the amount or way that someone worked), and 58% of trafficking victims noted an increase in fraud. Women experienced more force, fraud, and coercion than men. Workers who entered the industry as minors or who were homeless growing up were also more vulnerable to force, fraud, and coercion.

Why did so many workers receive more force, fraud, or coercion, and more contact by would-be traffickers? Participants frequently answered that because many forms of safe advertising (especially Backpage) had disappeared or were cracked down on, pimps and violent offenders posing as clients knew that workers were more vulnerable. Additionally, the disappearance of screening sites, or "blacklists," which allowed workers to identify and report bad clients to the sex work community, made it impossible to differentiate a safe client from a violent one. Pimps took advantage of this, claiming to be able to provide "protection." As one participant stated: "I had pimps attempting to stalk/harass/recruit me on social media dozens of times. I had actually never been contacted by one prior to FOSTA. They were trying to fly me out, get me to work for them, find out where I live, etc."

The loss of safe advertising and screening databases led to the loss of money, and an increase in people that were willing to exploit financial hardship to control workers.

FOSTA Created Dangerous Work Conditions, Increasing Violence and Exploitation

FOSTA not only increased sex trafficking and recruitment by pimps–it actively made the workplace more dangerous. Because many forms of safe advertising had disappeared, and because safe clients became more paranoid about giving out personal details commonly used in screening, workers lost their resources to vet clients for their safety. The results show that 39% of participants stated that they experienced more physical and sexual assault after FOSTA. For trafficking survivors, this was 67%, and for people with disabilities, it was 53%. Participants reported being robbed, raped, beaten, and locked into rooms. Yet, despite the increase in violence, workers were less likely to go to the police for assistance, because they were afraid of being arrested. FOSTA caused more harm for our most vulnerable groups while empowering and enabling violent perpetrators.

FOSTA also made work conditions more dangerous in other ways; largely because of increased financial hardship and more difficulty in finding reliable clients, 35% of participants had to lower their rates (44% of trafficking survivors and 46% of those with disabilities) and 41% started offering services that they were not comfortable with (47% of trafficking survivors and 52% of those with disabilities). Workers reported that clients pressured them to have sex without condoms or to participate in illicit drugs. Clients are demanding more services and lower rates, causing workers to have to see more clients and perform more services to support themselves and their dependents, increasing the risk that they are going to have a bad encounter.

FOSTA Increased Street-Based Sex Work

The loss of advertising and increased financial hardship after FOSTA forced many sex workers onto the streets. This report shows that 11% of participants who had not previously engaged in street-based work turned to it after the passage of FOSTA. That number was much higher for vulnerable groups–17% of trafficking survivors, 24% of those who entered the industry as minors, and 21% of people with disabilities turned to street-based work.

Street-based sex work is significantly more dangerous. Workers often do not have time to adequately vet their clients to ensure their own safety before getting in their cars. Being in a moving vehicle with child safety locks decreases a worker's safety. The driver has control, thus power to violate sex workers. Workers can rarely bring friends or security along with them for safety, and there can sometimes be more people in a car than expected. It is incredibly easy, then, for a bad encounter to happen, and street-based workers often have little they can do to prevent it. As one participant stated: "When working on any street, us workers are in danger from everyone. Whether it's teens driving by in a car, throwing baseballs and slurs at us; or it's the violent client kicked out of every club in town, coming to where he knows he's 'allowed to hurt women.' street-based sex work is so dangerous for the workers involved."

By forcing more workers onto the street, FOSTA puts more people (often young, homeless, and/or with a disability) in extreme danger, with no institutional safety nets to support them.

FOSTA Decreased Blacklist Access

Blacklists–community made databases that warn workers of unsafe clients–are vital to keeping workers safe. Especially when workers are traveling to new cities or do not have many regulars in an area, being able to identify whether a potential client is violent or otherwise dangerous before meeting with them in person is of the utmost importance.

Yet innumerable blacklists disappeared or were deleted after FOSTA. Prior to FOSTA, 68% of participants stated they used two or more blacklists. More vulnerable populations were more likely to use blacklists; 72% of trafficking survivors, 72% of people with disabilities, and 84% of people who entered the industry as minors used two or more blacklists. Immediately following FOSTA, only 39% of participants used two or more blacklists, and 38% of participants used no blacklists at all, dramatically increasing their risk. Trafficking survivors, people with disabilities, and people who entered the industry as minors were more likely to lose access to blacklists, increasing their nexus of vulnerability.

While access to blacklists has increased in the years since FOSTA, progress has been marginal, and many workers have nowhere near the same amount of access to blacklists that they had prior to FOSTA. Moreover, these new blacklists are often less comprehensive, as years of data have been wiped from the internet. Without reliable blacklists warning of rapists, robbers, or kidnappers, sex workers are in the dark about who they are meeting. Safety tools such as these are needed and necessary, and working without them can be terrifying for many.

One participant explained, "my access to blacklists disappeared so a lot of predators got a fresh slate."

FOSTA Made Screening Less Possible

In addition to blacklists, many workers who advertise online make use of other screening techniques, such as requiring a customer to email them from their work email address to prove their identity, checking court system databases for violent charges, or using other information provided by the client to look them up in various databases. This screening system relies on trust - because customers don't want to be arrested, they have to trust that any information about themselves that they send to an escort will be kept confidential and will not be intercepted by police. Events like FOSTA that increase customers' fear of police decrease their willingness to provide screening information.

Another formerly popular screening technique was to require a reference from another worker before meeting a new client. However, increased fear of police makes workers fearful of providing information about their clients to other workers and makes clients fearful of providing information about other escorts they've seen. Additionally, in many states, providing a reference for a client can be prosecuted as felony sex trafficking or promoting prostitution.

Prior to the passage of FOSTA, 51% of participants stated that they were always able to use screening procedures that made them feel safe, and an additional 26% stated that they were usually able to do so. Only 6% of participants never used screening procedures for their work. However, 78% of participants stated that FOSTA negatively impacted their ability to use screening procedures, and 15% of participants stated that after FOSTA they were no longer able to use safe screening procedures at all. Again, FOSTA increases the risks that workers undertake to stay financially stable, and loss of screening abilities harms already vulnerable groups: people with disabilities, people who entered the industry as minors, people who have been victimized within the industry, and those who experienced homelessness growing up.

FOSTA Decreased Community Support Among Sex Workers

After FOSTA, workers became fearful of being prosecuted for doing nothing more than helping keep other workers safe. As such, many sex workers felt uncomfortable or unsafe organizing with other workers. Seventy-one percent of participants stated that FOSTA hindered their willingness or ability to organize with other sex workers for safety purposes, ranging from outreach activities to community brunches. Vulnerable populations, including survivors of trafficking and those who had entered the industry as minors were even less willing to organize locally. Most concerningly, 43% of participants indicated that they were less likely to help a new worker that asked for safety tips. Many participants expressed fear that a worker reaching out for tips may be an informant, an undercover cop, or a violent offender looking to use those tips against them. As one worker stated: "Now I am screening those new workers just like I screen new clients. I need to know who they are before I interact. I fear that cops and informants are everywhere now. I used to be the first to mentor a new girl but not anymore, sorry to say."

Other participants expressed fear of being labeled a pimp if they provided assistance to new workers. For example, one commented, "the law can prosecute under FOSTA/SESTA for helping other full-service sex workers." Another wrote, "I cannot help other sex workers or do outreach publicly without the danger of being labeled a pimp." FOSTA is the first federal law that we know of since the Mann Act to expand the definition of pimping/trafficking to include standard prostitution practices. Now, not only will workers not seek police assistance if they are in danger, they also fear sharing potentially life-saving safety information with other sex workers. This results in decreased public safety and health.

Similarly, FOSTA prevented participants from organizing or attending a conference (42%), participating in online forums (58%), identifying as a sex worker in public advocacy for reform or legislative change (58%), and publishing articles, essays, and op-eds (31%). Survivors of trafficking, disabled persons, those who entered the industry as minors, and people of color were generally less willing or able than the average participant to identify publicly as a sex worker after FOSTA. The silencing effect of FOSTA prevents workers' stories and opinions from being heard, makes it less likely that public opinion or legislation will become more favorable to sex workers, and continues to criminalize workers' lives and livelihoods.

FOSTA Increased Homelessness

Because FOSTA has decreased our income and safety, many sex workers have lost their homes. 10% of participants reported homelessness due to FOSTA, and 28% experienced unstable housing. Survivors of trafficking, those with disabilities, and people of color were more likely to experience unstable housing (34, 37, and 40% respectively). While some were able to recover in the years since FOSTA, many were not. Of those who experienced homelessness or unstable housing in the wake of FOSTA, 20% were offered housing by a pimp, 43% were offered housing by someone trying to exploit them for free sex, 22% were denied services or discriminated against by homeless shelters because they were a sex worker, and 18% expressed that everything spiraled out of control, and they were never able to recover.

Those who entered the industry as minors had the lowest rates of relying on someone who was trying to exploit them for help, but the highest rates of being discriminated against at shelters. They also had the lowest rate of recovering from homelessness. Other vulnerable groups were impacted in different ways; survivors of trafficking were more likely to be contacted by a pimp, and persons with disabilities were particularly likely to be exploited or offered housing for free sex. As such, even those who were able to find housing after homelessness were not necessarily safe. As one participant stated: "Lost my housing due to lost work after FOSTA and inability to advertise. Bad housing situation now. Not safe or stable but it's better than homelessness. I'd rather stay living here where they take advantage of my disabilities and inability to move and often use coercion to get free work out of me than go to a pimp."

While losing a home is a devastating experience for anyone, it is especially difficult for sex workers. For workers who've had a prostitution charge, it can be impossible to rent a home - in some states, like Rhode Island, landlords who rent to known sex workers can be charged with felony Pandering or Sex Trafficking.

FOSTA Negatively Impacted Public Safety

Only 12 of the survey participants had reported a work-related crime to police since FOSTA passed. For 5 of them, FOSTA had no effect, but 7 of them reported that police were unable to subpoena information to aid in their investigation because FOSTA had moved websites overseas. For people of color who reported crimes to police - 5 of the 12 reports - FOSTA impeded all police investigations. While this small sample size indicates the rareness of sex workers turning to police for help, it also indicates that FOSTA is likely impeding at least half of investigations into sex work related crimes.

Survey participants were asked how FOSTA affected the likelihood of them reporting serious crimes to police. If they were assaulted at work, 70% said they are less likely to report to police because of FOSTA. One explained, "I no longer have as much info on who I see or ability to give contact points. The cops won't care, and it will open me to targets." If a client showed them child pornography, 50% said they are less likely to report to police because of FOSTA. Several participants left comments similar to this one: "I'm so sorry, really wish it were different and I would find a way to do something but walking into the police department myself wouldn't be it!" While FOSTA does not target individual sex workers reporting crimes to police, to sex workers it represented a significant increase in hostility towards them by the federal government and law enforcement community. This might explain why FOSTA so heavily impacted the likelihood of sex workers and sex trafficking survivors reporting serious crimes.

Individual sex workers may rarely or never be the victim or witness of a serious crime. It is also true that serial predators, who represent significant threats to public safety, target sex workers because they know we are afraid of police. It is in everyone's best interest to create policy that incentivizes the reporting and investigation of these kinds of predators in our communities.

FOSTA Harmed Survivors More

Survivors of force, fraud, or coercion within the sex industry and those who had entered the sex industry as minors faced more violence, exploitative work conditions, and vulnerability due to FOSTA than the larger group of survey participants. Their economic outcomes and recovery from homelessness were much worse.

Those who had been victims of force, fraud, or coercion within the industry faced the largest increases in violence: 64% - 24% more than all participants - reported more force and coercion within the industry after FOSTA, and 58% - 21% more than all participants - reported an increase in fraud within the industry after FOSTA. 67% - 22% more than all participants - reported an increase in violence by clients or those posing as clients, while 44%- 9% more than all participants - reported lowering their rates and 47% - 6% more than all participants - reported offering new services that they weren't comfortable with to survive the post-FOSTA market. Only

1% more of these survivors reported an increase in recruitment by pimps than the whole group of survey participants did. Those who are successfully targeted by sex traffickers are typically vulnerable people with multiple intersecting marginalized identities, and it is these same factors that make them more likely to be targets of and other kinds of violence.

Of those who had entered the industry as minors, 56% - 16% more than all participants - reported an increase in force and coercion within the industry after FOSTA, and 48% - 11% more than all participants - reported an increase in fraud within the industry. Fifty two percent - 13% more than all participants - reported an increase in violence from clients or those posing as clients. Those who entered the industry as minors lowered their rates less often than the rest of the survey participants and started offering new services that they were uncomfortable with only 1% more often.

Twenty four percent of those who entered the industry as minors reported turning to street-based work after FOSTA - more than twice the 11% of the larger group, and substantially more than the 17% of survivors of force, fraud, or coercion. Both groups reported elevated levels of FOSTA preventing them from organizing with other sex workers or communicating online.

Of those who became homeless or unstably housed due to FOSTA, 37% of those who entered the industry as minors - 19% more, or almost twice as much, as all participants - reported that everything spiraled out of control, and they still haven't recovered. The survey found that 63% - almost three times as much as the whole group - reported that they were discriminated against at shelters or other assistance programs, reducing public safety. When homeless, they relied on someone who was trying to exploit them for help five percent less than all participants, and 38% reported being offered free housing by a pimp, more than any other group.

Of those who had been victims of force, fraud, or coercion within the industry and become homeless or unstably housed due to FOSTA, 36% - 16% more than all participants - were offered housing by a pimp. 64% - that's 21% more than all participants - were offered housing by someone who was trying to exploit them, and 48% - 18% more than the whole group - accepted help from someone who was trying to exploit them.

Again, the same factors that make a person more vulnerable or likely to be targeted by sex traffickers also make them more likely to be discriminated against when accessing services or exploited when desperate for housing.

Men Were Less Impacted

Only 18 men took the survey, with only 15 completing it. More male survey participants would be needed to draw strong conclusions. Still, the differences are dramatic and warrant attention.

Only 13% of male sex workers and sex trafficking survivors reported an increase in violence from clients or those posing as clients after FOSTA - only a third as much as the whole group reported. Thirty one percent of male sex workers and sex trafficking survivors reported an increase in pressure to provide services they were uncomfortable with - a little more than half of the 54% of the whole group who did. They lowered their rates and began offering new services they were uncomfortable with 10% less than the whole group. None of them reported turning to street-based work after FOSTA. Their free speech and networks of support were also dramatically less impacted.

The subgroup of male sex workers and sex trafficking survivors who became homeless due to FOSTA is too small to draw any conclusions from, but the differences are again dramatic.

Differences in Impacts for Other Groups

While people of color had relatively similar responses throughout the survey, investigations of crimes they reported to police were more than twice as likely to be hindered by FOSTA. In fact, investigations of 100% of crimes reported by people of color were hindered by FOSTA, while only about half of investigations of crimes reported by other groups were hindered by FOSTA. Sex workers can be valuable partners in public safety, preventing and reporting serious crime. FOSTA allows sex traffickers, rapists, child pornographers, and other predators to commit these crimes without prosecution.

Thirty seven percent of survey participants reported having a disability, and were disproportionately impacted by FOSTA, with elevated rates of violence throughout and the highest percentage of lowering the rates for their services being forced by post-FOSTA conditions to offer services they were uncomfortable with. They turned to street-based work almost twice as often as the whole group, and reported the highest rates of homelessness and unstable housing. Further, those with disabilities had the highest rate of receiving new public assistance.

A major predictor of violence before and after FOSTA was homelessness growing up.

Resiliency and Distrust in Those Who Entered the Industry as Minors

Those who had entered the industry as minors and those who have been victims of force, fraud, or coercion within the industry are both defined federally as sex trafficking victims. While there is some overlap between the groups, the survey found some interesting differences in their experiences that can be summarized as worse experiences with "the system," more distrust of the system and other people, and more resilience in terms of pursuing income and avoiding potential predators.

While they were more likely than other participants to be victimized within the industry or by clients or those posing as clients, they were less likely to be victimized than those who had been victims of force, fraud, or coercion within the industry.

They lowered their rates less than other survey participants and were by far the most likely to turn to street-based work. They had the highest rates of blacklist usage, and if they became homeless, they were less likely than any other group (except men) to accept help from someone trying to exploit them, however they reported the worst outcomes after homelessness. They received less new public assistance after FOSTA but were denied public assistance more than any other group. They reported the highest rate of being unable to be financially secure with FOSTA in place.

They reported being less likely to report crimes to police because of FOSTA more than any other group and were the only group who wasn't significantly more likely to report child pornography than an assault on themselves. They reported being less likely to help another sex worker with safety information because of FOSTA at the highest rates, and also reported the highest rates of being reluctant or unable to express themselves online in a way that attracts customers who are looking for the sorts of services they provide because of FOSTA.

Vulnerability and Mutual Aid in Survivors Of FFC

Survivors of force, fraud, or coercion within the sex industry reported increased violence within the industry and from clients or those posing as clients at the highest rates. They were more likely than those who entered the industry as minors to lower their rates or start offering new services they weren't comfortable with. They reported using blacklists more than any other group other than those who entered the industry as minors but had the highest drop-in rate of blacklist accessibility after FOSTA.

They were more likely than any other group to help a new worker with safety information, more likely than any other group to report to police if they were assaulted, and most likely to accept help from someone who was trying to exploit them if they became homeless. These numbers may reflect less bad experiences with "the system" and more trust in other people.

Other Interesting Demographics

Entry to the sex industry:

- 93% reported entering the industry willingly.

- 2% reported being forced or coerced to enter the industry.

- 5% reported being tricked or manipulated into entering the industry.

- 10% reported entering the industry as a minor.

Work conditions:

- 77% reported having worked independently without being victimized.

- 66% reported having worked with others without being victimized.

- 14% reported having been a victim of force or coercion within the industry.

- 16% reported having been a victim of lies or manipulation within the industry.

Of the transgender people who took the survey (34) a little more than half (18) use a cisgendered persona for work.

37% of survey participants reported having a disability.

26% of survey participants reported experiencing homelessness growing up.

Stories Participants Shared

We asked if participants had any stories about the effects of FOSTA that they wanted to share with policy makers. Here are some of the responses:

> *"Exiting sex work has become significantly less viable because I am never in a position to save money after the income drop."*

"Mostly my friends with tentative document status are affected. They really try to stay under the radar."

"FOSTA made safety screening impossible and illegal. It's terrifying how lawmakers don't care about our safety even though the effects of FOSTA were clearly predicted by those in the industry."

"All you did was prevent women like me, who have made the choice willingly from making an income. Of those that are truly trafficked all you did was push it further underground and you can't help them, if you can't see them. This was the most stupid inconsiderate law of those that are truly trafficked. I've been a working girl since 1987 and not once have I encountered someone that's been trafficked."

"As somebody who was trafficked, it's incredibly insensitive that lawmakers pushed this kind of thing under the guise of lowering traffic. All it did was remove a degree of separation for safety that we use and push more providers into the arms of traffickers and pimps. The hypocrisy is unreal. They don't care about us, it's just about control. And I could tell you many stories about the Republicans that have come to me for my services but still support FOSTA."

"Before FOSTA, there was a whole network of experienced workers who could help newbies learn about things like screening, deposits, blacklists, etc. You took all that away, so now people are even more vulnerable to predators."

"Before FOSTA I mostly worked at massage parlors and felt so much safer working with others and knowing that there was always at least 1-2 other people looking out for

me. It became decidedly more dangerous to work with others (particularly in the same physical space) after FOSTA so I've only worked solo since then and ultimately had to quickly transition to full service/escorting full time."

"When I tried to submit my ad on Backpage and saw that it was shut down, I had to start stripping and saw customers from the strip club instead. But, since it was in person I wasn't able to screen them as well so it was a lot more dangerous."

"In Seattle we saw a direct correlation between websites being shutdown after FOSTA and strip clubs being flooded with displaced sex workers and clients. This work conditions in the strip clubs to become imbalanced and less profitable for strippers. Safety decreased as clients from websites tried to get services that strippers didn't supply. As a result, strippers organized and passed legislation to increase safety in the clubs, but this did not address the imbalanced caused by displaced sex workers."

"1. A woman I know was working out of town when all the sites went down. Because she couldn't advertise herself she started working with an agency. The agency sent her to see a man at a casino who assaulted her and took all her money. The police said they could only arrest him for assault if they also arrested her for prostitution. She was stuck in this faraway city with no money and her face was all bruised up so she couldn't work even if there was a way for her to get clients. 2. Another woman I know was living day to day in a cheap hotel. Within two days of all the sites coming down she was outside in the cold trying to find customers. She became homeless and lived in a tent for

over a year. 3. After FOSTA I traveled to a rural oil boom town I sometimes work in. I found that a couple pimps had abandoned several sex workers each in this little town. They had no money to leave or pay for their rooms or find new customers and customers knew it. Most of them started offering bareback services for half of their normal rate just to make the money to get out of town. I can't imagine how many STIs were transmitted. Because bbfs for $100 was the new standard there, I made no money and was lucky that I had the money to travel home and still pay my bills."

"I have a friend who was put out on the street by her pimp when the websites fell. The very first night she was robbed and raped at gun point. When she got back to her pimp, he beat her because her money was stolen. She had never experienced this before and kept telling me how out of control she felt. Another friend called me and told me she was going to choose up. (Get a pimp) because she was losing her home."

"I have been kicked off of social media platforms for even attempting to discuss rights related to sex work."

"One of the street-based POC trans sex workers I advocate for lost her housing as a result of FOSTA. When she lost her housing and started doing street sex work was raped brutally by a client and now has HIV because of the rape. When I started working with her she was being repeatedly exploited. We were able to get her interim housing but she is sick and now disabled. She still does sex work to survive but cannot disclose her status for fear of being beaten or killed. Thank you FOSTA. "

"The bottom line is digitally discriminating and deplatforming sex workers is an act of violence. Not listening or collaborating with the very communities you are writing policy about has life altering repercussions for said communities and those apart of them. Some of us are being forced into more dangerous lines of work because we cannot work safely online or utilize safe working practices such as screening or Decriminalization. It's unacceptable and sex workers need protections now. Our voices have been left out of policy and legislation for too long, we don't need legislators speaking for us when we have voices. It's time to start collaborating with sex workers and reflecting our needs in everyday life. Sex work is work and we need human rights."

"A good friend who had made his income using ads online had all his ads taken down and immediately had to stay in a house with people who triggered his addiction. I had three different SWers stay with me while they tried to figure out new ways to bring in income and had lost their housing. Also, the level of anxiety and feeling scared, hunted, oppressed, run down, and burnt out just skyrocketed. I've seen a LOT of people who were ground down in the past few years because of how hard it is to get good clients now, and some of them ended up taking their own lives. The mental health toll has been astronomical."

"FOSTA put the power in the hands of pimps and exploitative clients. Taking away online platforms means not being able to set prices in advance and sometimes having to argue with clients in the moment."

"Because she was unable to advertise for or screen new clients, my sister was forced to move in with a client to have shelter. The client took her to Hawaii under the guise of a getaway vacation, but abandoned her there without her shoes, phone, or ID. She was homeless for 6 months before we could find her and get her. She died a month after she came home from suicide."

"A client hired me and wanted to show me child pornography. I said no and asked him if he was concerned about FOSTA/SESTA increasing his risk of being prosecuted. He laughed at me. It was chilling. "Now it's even easier, " he said. "We have our own code and still get what we want, we have our own networks without websites." I didn't report it because I was afraid I would be arrested for being with the client to come to the knowledge in the first place. Other people online have used the law to increase harassment, threats and deplatforming for me. I just want to do my job and have a peaceful life with my family."

"He saw my ads online. I didn't know he knew. I took my car to the garage for my appointment...when I got it back the air conditioner was broken, I had severe asthma, and the headlights had been intentionally shorted out. The appointment was for an oil change and to fix a part in the driver's side window mechanism. There was no need to be near the headlights or the air conditioner. He then spent months sexually extorting me, sharing my photos with his friends at work, coercing me to make illegal content in Pennsylvania and promising to fix my car. I took it to a BMW mechanic who said the damage done to my

headlights would cost over $5,000 to fix. I couldn't afford that. It was a big mess. I tried to call the owner of the garage, I just wanted my car fixed, and they laughed claiming I'd be the one arrested for prostitution. And he was not wrong. The cops wouldn't even have investigated him...they likely would have arrested me. FOSTA/SESTA didn't help end sex trafficking, it made sex workers and non sex workers more susceptible to violence. I lost over $4,000 when I had to trade my car in 7 months after the abuse started. It was the only way I could end the abuse and still survive. No car = no work = no survival."

"Not being able to keep platforms keeps you behind in not only organizing but also groups to get involved in. It feels more dangerous to self-identify even in academic or organizer spaces because of whats going on online."

"There's not many forums where you can connect with other sexworkers. Having a connected community keeps us together and safe and we need to connect with likeminded adults because like LGBQ we hold a stigma with people who don't understand our life choices. It can get very lonely."

"I used to be a lot more outspoken about sex worker's rights online, but ever since FOSTA, I've been wary about referencing the work so explicitly. I tiptoe around topics I would much prefer to just speak openly about."

"I lost my home, my savings, everything. I was forced to move back home with a family who was abusive because I had no other options until I was able to get a factory job and save up my money and then head out to a brothel so I

can get back on my feet. Going to the brothel was a very awful experience, the one that I went to there was a lot of drama that ensued and it was not a safe place. I was able to move down the road to another brothel, save my money and eventually make my way back to San Francisco. My life has been a wreck since FOSTA. I do not work well with the public, I also prefer staying home, and working from home on my own schedule was how I enjoyed my life."

"Last month [an] escort who had quit screening her clients after FOSTA, was robbed and the man punched out both of her front teeth. As soon as I arrived on the scene I asked her if she wanted to make a police report and she said no. She told me that a few years before she caught a prostitution case and DCYF threatened to take her kids and made her jump through all kinds of hoops to keep her kids and it took her almost 2 years to have that case closed."

"I used to share helpful information about sex work and sex worker issues before FOSTA. Doing so after FOSTA resulted in social media accounts being disabled and shadow banned."

"I worked in hotels on backpage and was a good girl with really good clients. When they took that down I didn't know what to do. I am disabled with a traumatic brain injury so I'm not working a real job."

"Conditions became extremely unsafe and definitely made it less likely for myself or others to help."

"We have been targeted by social media platforms for censorship, even when our expression does not violate any

of the platform's terms of service. It's harder to share safety information, harder to warn others of active predators, and harder to have a normal, non-sex-work related social media presence."

"I stopped working in a secure location and had to move around to avoid the risk of suspicion. It cost more in overhead. See fewer clients. Less income."

"When FOSTA first hit, it directly caused the deaths of half a dozen sex workers (that I heard of via Twitter). That a law that was supposed to "save" us only created literal victims should be proof that criminalization does not work."

"Just talking about sex work can get you suspended from social media, financial institutions like PayPal or Bank of America can close your account, landlords can put you on the street."

"I grew up in an abusive and isolated religious cult, which forced me into homelessness at 15yo. This abandonment from my family and community resulted in years of homelessness, sexual abuse, and substance abuse. After getting sober, I tried desperately to retain steady employment, and housing, but with my lack of education due to being raised in a religious cult which refused adequate education, and having no family or community support, keeping employment that covered my bills was not possible, especially when I tried to go to college. I ended up having to drop out, and ultimately lost my employment due to trying to juggle financially self-supporting, and education. I entered the sex work industry at the age of 20

years old (2013), when I lost my decent job, and was 2 months late on rent. I was applying to jobs nonstop for 2 months, but the only response I got was a Craigstlist ad, which turned out to be a body rub agency. I made my 2 months rent in the span of less than a week, and I was finally back on track with my bills! I worked with the industry for a short time, but after experiencing a few violent interactions with clients who the industry lied about screening, I figured out how to advertise, and went independent. When the lease on my room ended a few months later however, I was unable to prove my income for a new apartment, and went on to experience housing insecurity, as well as exploitative/dangerous housing for 1 year, until I was finally able to find someone to be a guarantor for an apartment, and I got my own place (2015) - This guarantor "favor" ended up being an attempt at exploitation, which later (2017) caused me to experience housing insecurity once again, when the attempt at exploitation was denied. I was also sexually assaulted by a client for a loan to cover the massive downpayment required for that apartment, because I did not have traditional proof of income. During the 1.5 years that I was able to retain stable housing, I was experiencing a lot of PTSD. This resulted in an attempt to leave the industry, get a day job, and go back to college, which ultimately proved unsuccessful, and I was back to housing insecurity (Summer 2016). This is when I re-entered the industry. I was very inexperienced with technology. Even though I had left the religious cult years ago, and finally had access to secular reading material, and the internet, I could never afford a computer, or modern smart devices, and was very socially isolated. This made growing in the industry, and

more financial security than I ever have, but I want to discuss the few challenges that I experience in this industry that are directly related to FOSTA. 1. Advertising is astronomically expensive. If I'm not doing amazing financially, I have to weigh eating, and advertising. Advertising in a large city can cost a whopping $800/month for just 1 website. Now post FOSTA, getting clients usually requires advertising on at least 3. 2. Free platforms like social media often include being shadowbanned for months at a time, and having accounts shut down, causing a loss of work for months, and thousands of dollars. 3. Due to the changes in advertising platforms, it has been harder to advertise anonymously, this meant sacrificing my anonymity and having my photos used all over the internet without my consent, making it much harder to have future prospects outside of this industry if I want to move on to something else. This also risks my tender relationship with my family. 4. Screening and blacklisting boards are still very limited. This means having stricter screening requirements, limiting clients I can see, and for others who can't afford to turn clients away, being put into dangerous situations. 5. I have been fortunate to be able to shift from survival work to "high-end" work, however, I have spent upwards of 30k over the last few years to make that possible. This has significantly hindered my ability to build long-term financial security. I can't write off expenses that any other non-sex work business could. 6. I have very limited options for accepting deposits securely. Deposits can be another form of screening, and limits our liabilities for travel, time, and expenses. (Without deposits clients are unreliable, and can cancel or no show, costing the provider money in prep time, travel, and other expenses)."

"I was the victim of a pimp in my first year of sex work. There was no correlation with FOSTA. The only factor in my vulnerability to this kind of abuse was that I was new and isolated. Since getting out of that situation I have been able to find community & safety in the industry. I would not consider myself in danger of experiencing anything like that again. "

"It was a really scary, anxious time when FOSTA passed. I remember having panic attacks and suicidal ideation because I was afraid I was going to lose my livelihood. I had just bought a house for the first time and was trying to get out of an unhealthy relationship, and was terrified I wouldn't be able to pay for my mortgage or the renovations that were already underway. I remember spending hours reviewing my Twitter feed, deleting any tweets that referred to "sex work" because many of us were afraid we'd have our accounts shut down, which we rely on for advertising and marketing. I cried a lot because I felt like I was losing an important part of my identity and my online expression. I used to be a lot more outspoken about sex worker's rights online, but ever since FOSTA, I've been wary about referencing the work so explicitly. I tiptoe around topics I would much prefer to just speak openly about. There was a lot of administrative trouble that came with FOSTA because of elevated concerns around online privacy. Like many full service workers who advertise online, I switched all my email communication from Gmail to encrypted email and began requiring clients to only correspond using an encrypted email address themselves. It has often been a huge administrative headache to try to convince ignorant clients who are unaware of the risks of FOSTA to set up

new email addresses, and then remember to check their inboxes. I have lost thousands and thousands of dollars in potential work because of clients forgetting to check their encrypted email accounts. I also moved all of my domain registration offshore as another security precaution and started using VPNs religiously to protect my privacy online. I am much more vigilant about online privacy as a result of FOSTA and worry more about potential legal repercussions around basic things that are necessary to make my living. Like many of my colleagues, I took down my duo / friends page (a page on my website that profiled friends I enjoy working with) because it could be perceived as (now felony-level) trafficking. I feel like the industry used to be much more social and more collaborative before the fear instilled in us by FOSTA, which put a stop to a lot of community events and online connections. And shadowbanning has become a huge problem on Twitter, which reduces the visibility of our accounts and impacts our income. It's not clear why this happens, but there is certainly a pattern of escorts' PG-rated tweets being buried / hidden for no apparent reasons. Overall, I've been very lucky and privileged among sex workers as a whole. I'm highly educated, white, able bodied, conventionally attractive. I still make 6 figures annually, can afford to own a house, travel, pursue continuing education, while trying to build a secondary business. But I feel censored by FOSTA and have heightened privacy and security concerns in a way that I didn't before, and I'm sad to have lost the sense of community and collaboration that was more common before FOSTA passed. And I worry endlessly about additional bills inspired by FOSTA and so-called anti-trafficking, anti-money laundering efforts that could cause my bank accounts or payment processing to get shut down, which would effectively destroy my business and my ability to make a living. I have had to learn how to navigate the (expensive) world of cryptocurrency, just to be able to pay for my online ads, because banks and credit card companies are scrutinizing accounts more (which I think is indirectly connected to the legal climate FOSTA has created) and I fear my accounts being shut down for using my credit card. I believe FOSTA has also contributed to the loss of prepaid Visa cards as an option for paying for ad sites, which many of us used to do in order to protect our privacy. Ad sites are also requiring more and more proof of identity to protect themselves, which is another privacy/security risk for workers, and makes me quite nervous. Despite my relative stability and privilege within this risky industry, everything feels much more precarious than before FOSTA and that is very, very unfortunate. And to think that so many workers are much worse off than me, have died to be left homeless or forced to return to street work and be exploited by pimps, directly as a result of FOSTA, is just devastating."

"Fosta took away backpage which at the time was a major resource to advertise and find clients . Providers living day by day were devastated and our futures were unknown leaving us in hurt and confusion."

"If policy makers want to stop trafficking, they have got to make the work safer for independent workers. When independent workers feel under threat from law enforcement, we are not going to risk helping the new girl

*who is unknown. Without our help she *will* fall under the control of a pimp and be exploited."*

"I'm a single mother. I have court order child support that's never paid or collected. I am raising the children completely on my own with no help and I'm struggling worse than I ever was. I was 25 when I started working in the massage parlors and now I'm 50 and I plan to be here for another 25 years as I don't have any other choice. Signed SWSWM SINGLE WHITE SEX WORKING MOM."

"I currently live gig to gig instead of having a financial safety net since fosta/sesta."

"As a result of FOSTA, one of my colleagues had her income plummet. The house she owned went into foreclosure, and she eventually lost it. Working hard to put her life back together, she rented out a small apartment. She still has to make hard decisions between paying a bill or refilling prescriptions."

"My business at the brothel dropped to virtually nothing and the madam became even more paranoid and controlling, all of which prompted me to work as an independent provider. On the whole, I've been much happier, healthier, and more prosperous on my own."

"I am severely mentally ill. I'm under care but unable to function in normal society for long periods of time. I need to be able to do this. I'm good for short bursts. I have been denied disability despite doctors' recommendations."

"Not only was my life, my safety, my voice, and my ability to speak freely on social media threatened or at risk. But the lives of my Fellow workers in the industry that I know across America, and in other countries as well. I know women who've had to resort to doing things they've never wanted to do to survive, because they have children to take care of, or themselves. I know woman who've been beaten and robbed and raped just like me. I know women who've had to flee the country to find work in other countries, only to face similar dangers and stigma in a new place. If you care about sex workers, you will repeal FOSTA/SESTA. Both of these bills target us, are based in stigma and whorephobia, and harm working citizens. FOSTA/SESTA has done absolutely NOTHING to save or aid the lives of women and young girls who are being trafficked against their will. Consensual sex work and sex trafficking are two completely different things. Bills like this only conflate them, and kill or ruin the lives of working women in the process. There is a way to save victims of human trafficking, and it is not targeting consensual sex workers!"

"I had difficulty making ends meet, got offers from wannabe pimps, and had to work harder to attract good clients."

"I can't afford to have a social media presence or personal website so clients confirm my identity as a worker through reviews. After a grueling time under my latest work persona at a rate I didn't like with clients I didn't like, I finally became established enough via reviews that I could increase my rate and go back to a city I preferred. Then

FOSTA hit. I had no choice but to keep seeing my old clients, including a rapist and other boundary crossers, at less than half of what I wanted to charge (and used to charge under a previous persona.) I had to travel to see clients I did not like in this one particular city. I had to work more hours because of the low rate. I had no choice, because all my reviews were deleted after FOSTA and this was leveraged against me by prospective clients."

"Before Fosta, I was ok. I could pay all my bills, I had stable housing and clients who I could screen. When Fosta came into law, I lost everything. I lost my clients and my advertising platforms that let me work indoors and safely when I wanted to. I was desperate and pimps were the only ones who promised me an out, an option that would let me survive and do well. I paid in blood and tears for the money. I was forced to take clients they chose, and to offer services they wanted because I couldn't find my own clients."

Recommendations

* Repeal FOSTA/SESTA

Chapter 11: US Survey: Sexual Health

"People involved in the sex industry are people who are able to make healthy decisions about our bodies and take our health seriously just as anyone else. We deserve respect and bodily autonomy."

Survey Participant

Key Findings

* Sex workers are much more likely to use prophylaxis methods (like condoms and PrEP) than the general public.

* Many respondents highlighted the stigmas around sex work and STI / HIV status as making frequent testing more difficult to access, sometimes being required by healthcare providers to disclose or otherwise justify why they would want more frequent testing or preventative medicine.

* Most respondents described having easy access to quality reproductive care but this number was significantly lower for trans sex workers, who described decreased access and lower quality in their reproductive care provision.

* Approximately 1% of respondents were HIV positive, and about 0.13% had been diagnosed with AIDS. Thirteen percent of HIV positive respondents were receiving treatment.

* Forty-two percent of all respondents said that they had access to PrEP, while 41% said that they are not aware of what PrEP is. Eight percent of respondents use PrEP.

Introduction

This chapter describes sex workers' experiences with sexual health and reproductive medical care as shared in the US national survey created by COYOTE RI. It reviews the quantitative data from this survey and discusses the qualitative findings and recommendations given directly by respondents. Stigma and misinformation around sexual health contribute to harmful and inaccurate portrayals of sex workers as more likely to contribute to sexual diseases and infections, but findings suggest that sex workers are much more educated and proactive about sexual health than the general public. This chapter aims to provide accurate information on sex workers' sexual health experiences, including those with the healthcare system, as shared through their own words.

Sexually Transmitted Infection Testing and Condom Use

Eighty-two percent of respondents said that they get tested for sexually transmitted infections (like HIV, STI, HEP C, etc.) at least once a year or more (34% said they tested every three months, 26% every six months, and 22% once a year). This is significantly higher than the 20-37% nationally who report getting tested regularly.[2] Only 4% of survey respondents had never been tested,

---

[2]Hims&Hers. 2021. "Men's Health Research." https://www.hims.com/forhims/image/upload/v1622078041/
Hims_Men_s_Health_Online_Survey_Key_Data.pdf. Accessed June 2024.
Pediatrics 2022 "Annual STI Testing Among Sexually Active Adolescents" https://www.ncbi.nlm.nih.gov/pmc/articles/PMC9126309/

compared to the national average of 19%.[3] Approximately 13% of respondents who do not test regularly cited limited or no access to testing for STIs as the reason they do not get tested. This was slightly higher for sex workers of color (16%) and trans sex workers (33%), although the number of respondents in this category were small. Most other responses cited not testing more regularly due to the type and frequency of sexual activity (not engaging in sex or other sexual contact with clients) or shifting frequency of testing depending on the type of sex work they are engaging in at that time.

Many respondents highlighted the stigmas around sex work, perceived frequent sexual activity or "promiscuity," and/or STI and HIV status as a contributing factor to making frequent testing more difficult to access, sometimes being required by healthcare providers to disclose or otherwise justify why they would want more frequent testing or preventative medicine. One respondent said "If we go in wanting to be proactive about things, such as testing or getting on Truvada, please just help us. Don't assume we're hiding additional risks or exposure to HIV and AIDS. And stop lumping in sex for money with sex for drugs. Or asking us questions about how many people we've had sex with during that testing period. Just let us get tested." Another person noted: "Let anyone who wants it take Truvada to protect themselves without asking why they need it or invasive questions about any partners they may have."

---

[3] LetsGetChecked. 2019. "Almost 50% of U.S. Adults Don't Know How Often You Should Take an STD Test." https://www.letsgetchecked.com/articles/half-of-us-adults-dont-know-how-often-you-should-take-an-std-test-std-survey/. Accessed June 2024.

Seventy-eight percent of respondents described always (59%) or often (19%) using condoms, only 9% said they never do. Many of those who described never using condoms specified that they do not engage in full-service sex work and do not use protection for no contact work. This 78% of sex workers using condoms regularly starkly compares to the national average of 17% of sexually active adults in the US who regularly use condoms in a six-month period.[4] Less than one percent of survey respondents described having no access to safe sex materials. More than half of respondents (52%) always use condoms even if the client is long-standing, while some (15%) made a few exceptions and others (10%) said it depends on the client. Seventy-two percent of respondents said that they have not worked without a condom even if there was more money involved in the negotiation, while 28% had. Many respondents used condoms in their social sexual relationships, though these numbers were lower than condom use in sex work and more evenly distributed in frequency. Respondents used condoms in personal relationships always (20%), often (23%), sometimes (20%), rarely (16%), or never (20%).

Birth Control and Reproductive Health Access

Ninety percent of respondents described having easy access to reproductive care, including condoms, birth control, fertility treatments, etc. Forty-one percent of respondents use medically prescribed birth control methods, while 59% do not. This was lower for sex workers of color (33% of whom used prescribed

---

[4] Nasrullah M, Oraka E, Chavez PR, Johnson CH, DiNenno E. 2017. "Factors Associated with Condom Use Among Sexually Active US Adults, National Survey of Family Growth, 2006-2010 and 2011-2013." Journal of Sexual Medicine. 14(4):541-550. doi: 10.1016/j.jsxm.2017.02.015. PMID: 28364979; PMCID: PMC5477642.

birth control) and trans sex workers (15% used prescribed birth control; 85% did not).

Eighty-four percent of respondents who use family planning clinics said that these clinics provided quality care for their reproductive needs. This number was noticeably lower for trans sex workers, only 50% of whom described quality reproductive care from family planning clinics. Fifty-two percent of respondents described having reliable access to sex-worker friendly health services. However, only 36% of respondents said that they tell their healthcare provider that they are a sex worker. (This is further discussed in healthcare service access in Chapter 10.)

HIV Status, Treatment, and PrEP

Approximately 1% of all respondents were HIV positive and 0.13% had been diagnosed with AIDS. Six percent of trans sex workers were HIV positive (n=35), but none of these respondents had been diagnosed with AIDS. Fifteen percent of HIV positive respondents had an undetectable HIV status. Laws criminalizing HIV or other STI exposure exist in some form in 34 states, and some states have laws making prostitution by HIV positive people a felony. These laws are criticized as undermining public health efforts to identify and address HIV, as well as compounding criminalization of sex workers.[5]

On December 1st (World AIDS Day) of 2023 the US Department of Justice found that the State of Tennessee violated the Americans

---

[5] Aziza Ahmed, Sienna Baskin & Anna Forbes. 2016. "Criminal Laws on Sex Work and HIV Transmission: Mapping the Laws, considering the Consequence." Denver Law Review 355(93). https://scholarship.law.bu.edu/faculty_scholarship/3102.

with Disabilities Act by enforcing its aggravated prostitution statute against people living with HIV. "Tennessee's aggravated prostitution law is outdated, has no basis in science, discourages testing and further marginalizes people living with HIV," said Assistant Attorney General Kristen Clarke of the Justice Department's Civil Rights Division. "People living with HIV should not be treated as violent sex offenders for the rest of their lives solely because of their HIV status. The Justice Department is committed to ensuring that people with disabilities are protected from discrimination.[6]"

Thirteen percent of general HIV positive respondents were receiving treatment, while 50% of HIV positive trans workers were receiving treatment. Fourteen percent of general positive respondents received their HIV care through private clinics; 38% through healthcare clinics; and 49% from other providers. Most (61%) felt that they were receiving adequate HIV healthcare, though sex workers of color reported the lowest numbers (53%) here.

Pre-exposure prophylaxis (or PrEP) is medicine taken to prevent contracting HIV. Forty-two percent of all respondents said that they had access to PrEP, while 41% said that they were not aware of what PrEP is. Eight percent of respondents use PrEP and 5% had partners who use PrEP, compared to approximately 0.01% of

---

[6] US Department of Justice "Justice Department Finds that Enforcement of Tennessee State Law Discriminates Against People with HIV." https://justice.gov/opa/pr/justice-department-finds-enforcement-tennessee-state-law-discriminates-against-people-hiv

the US population who are prescribed PrEP.[7]   Sixty-three percent of these found that PrEP had been effective for them. Sixty-six percent of all respondents said their medical provider had not discussed PrEP; 16% had discussed it with their medical provider in detail (9% in passing). Trans respondents were more likely to know what PrEP is (only 22% did not know), to have discussed it with their medical provider in detail (46%) or in passing (13%), to have access to PrEP (59%), to use PrEP (28%) or have a partner who uses PrEP (11%), and to have found it to be effective (88%).

Policy Insights

- Provide education to healthcare providers and the general public about the stigma around sex work and HIV. Healthcare providers should be trained and equipped to remain professional and supportive and not engage in moralistic judgment that impacts the healthcare provision they offer or include.

- Provide free access to healthcare, preventative medicine, and treatment for STIs and HIV. Increase the number of facilities and healthcare providers that can provide these aspects of medical care, specifically those supportive of sex workers.

- Repea prostitution by people living with HIV laws and HIV transmission laws, which further marginalize and criminalize HIV positive sex workers and can incentivize

---

[7] Lindsey Dawson, Brittni Frederiksen, and Ivette Gomez. 2022. "PrEP Access in the United States: The Role of Telehealth." https://www.kff.org/hivaids/issue-brief/prep-access-in-the-united-states-the-role-of-telehealth/#:~:text=The%20Centers%20for%20Disease%20Control,indicated%20need%20for%20the%20medication. Accessed June 2024.

workers to avoid HIV and STI testing. Prostitution laws that treat those with HIV differently from other sex workers may violate the Americans with Disabilities Act

Chapter 12: The Sex Industry and COVID-19

"I haven't seen any clients. But, I find it irritating that they keep contacting me to see when I am going to work again when we are all still at risk to spread Covid-19. And that they aren't really concerned about my safety and welfare."

Survey Participant

Key Findings

- The COVID-19 pandemic has negatively impacted the financial circumstances of many sex workers.

- 30% of respondents felt that the stigmatization of sex work has been exacerbated due to the pandemic.

- 60% of the respondents reported that they are not still taking clients in person, only 2% reported that they are taking in-person clients because they believe the coronavirus is a conspiracy theory, 10% reported taking in-person clients because they are not high risk, and 29% reported taking in-person clients because they have no other options.

Introduction

In Spring of 2020, the world saw one of the biggest global crises in the history of humankind, that crisis is known as the COVID-19 pandemic. During this time, COYOTE RI was in the process of producing this book. Given how the coronavirus has disproportionately affected marginalized groups and communities, we thought it important to survey sex workers during this global crisis and include this vital information shared by 189 research participants in this book.

Prior to (and during) the COVID-19 pandemic, sex workers were stigmatized and criminalized in the United States, making them more vulnerable to a global crisis. The pandemic has further exacerbated this stigmatization of sex work and put sex workers in precarious economic situations. Unlike others who have lost their jobs or been unable to work during the pandemic that are able to file for unemployment and receive benefits under the CARE Act, sex workers are unable to file their work since sex work is not considered real work federally.

In order to effectively care for all groups of people during a global pandemic, the government needs to listen to the voices and needs of those groups that are most marginalized. That is why we have reached out to sex workers to get their feedback, better understand their individual situations during this crisis, and listen to any recommendations they may have for policies that could better address the needs of those in precarious situations due to the pandemic.

Demographics

As this was a separate survey from the rest of the surveys conducted for this book, it is important to understand the demographics of the data we will be discussing in this section. The geographic distribution of participants was primarily along the East and West coast, with significantly fewer participants from the midwest and other regions. The largest numbers of participants were from Rhode Island (17%) and California (17%), with the next largest group of participants being located in Florida (7%), Washington (7%), and Massachusetts (6%).

Additionally, an overwhelming majority of participants were white (79%), 11% were multiracial, 2% were Black, and 2% were Asian. 71% of participants were ciswomen, 10% were nonbinary, 7% agender, 5% cis men, 5% trans women, and 1% trans men. In terms of sexual orientation, 33% were heterosexual, 24% were bisexual, 17% queer, 13% pansexual, 7% homosexual, 3% demisexual, and 1% asexual.

Given the nature of the survey, we were also interested in participants underlying health conditions and knowledge of public health procedures and advice. Twenty percent of respondents reported that yes they have underlying health conditions that do increase their risk of contracting COVID-19, while 19% reported yes, but it does not increase their likelihood of contracting COVID-19. Fifty three percent of respondents reported that they have no underlying health conditions or disabilities and 7% reported no, but that they are at risk due to their age or another factor. When asked if they have been able to follow social distancing and public health guidelines outside of work, 52% reported that they always were able to do so, 37% reported that they were usually able to do so, 8% reported sometimes, 1% reported rarely, and 2% reported they were never able to do so. The participants were then asked whether or not they have reviewed any harm reduction material regarding the transmission of COVID-19 through sex or intimacy. 56% reported that yes they had received information from the sex work community, while 26% had received it from the sex-positive community, 21% from the government, and 13% from the queer community. Only 27%

reported that no, they had received no information regarding the transmission of COVID-19 through sex or intimacy. When asked whether or not the respondents had successfully been able to access COVID-19 testing, 76% reported that they had not attempted to get tested, 14% tried and did get tested, while 8% tried and could not get tested.

Financial Inquiries

Next, we inquired about the participants' financial circumstances prior and during the COVID-19 pandemic to get a better sense of if and how the pandemic has caused a financial burden for sex workers. Prior to COVID-19, 66% reported that they did not have trouble making ends meet financially, while 34% did. After the outbreak of COVID-19 the number of participants that reported having difficulty making ends meet financially jumped to 78%. We then gave participants the opportunity to elaborate on how their financial burdens have been affected by COVID-19. Many noted that they were unable to work anymore, that they were relying on unemployment checks, that they are still seeing clients but are having to charge much less, that they have had to turn to work in the streets, that they are having trouble finding clients, that there is practically no work available and thus zero income, and that they have had to rely on charity or outside assistance to make ends meet.

We then inquired about whether or not the participants have health insurance and found that 73% did have health insurance while the remaining 27% did not. Prior to the outbreak of COVID-19, 77% of respondents were the sole providers of their families while only 22% were not. During the pandemic that number dropped to 71% of the respondents being the sole providers of their families and

28% not. About half of the respondents only support a household of 1, with 28% reporting 2, 15% reporting 3, and very few responding that they support a household of more than 3.

During the pandemic, many states instituted temporary bans on evictions, so we inquired about whether or not respondents reside in states that have instituted such policies. 61% responded that yes their state had suspended evictions, 17% responded no, and 22% were unsure. As seen from the graph above, the ability of people to pay bills, including housing bills, during the pandemic has been extremely strained, so instating such measures as this helps to ensure that people are able to make ends meet during the accentuating circumstances caused by the pandemic.

When asked about the COVID-19 stimulus checks from the federal government, 55% reported they had already received some of the stimulus checks, while 23% reported that they expected to. We then inquired about unemployment benefits: 68% of the respondents noted that they were aware of the unemployment benefits under the CARE Act, with 40% of the respondents reporting that they had applied for unemployment, 9% had not done so yet but planned to, 44% reported that no they had not with no plans to do so, while the remaining 7% reported no and then were given the capacity to elaborate. Some reasons they provided include having another job and not technically being unemployed or not being able to prove past work, such as sex work. Of those that reported having applied for unemployment, only 29% were approved, with some reporting that they did not know yet or planned to appeal the denial.

Although measures such as bans on evictions have been helpful to those struggling with finances during the pandemic, oftentimes federal policies fail to adequately provide for those in need or allow some marginalized groups to fall through the cracks. Mutual aid networks have been a major source of support in place of more formal aid from the federal or state governments for people during the pandemic, so we also inquired about whether or not any of the respondents had utilized mutual aid for financial support after the outbreak of COVID-19. 66% responded that they had not, 18% noted yes they received aid from a sex worker mutual aid fund, 9% received help from an informal community based mutual aid network, 7% received aid from a non-sex worker specific mutual aid fund, while 10% reported "other".

Next, we wanted to know more about the respondent's individual financial situations during the pandemic as they relate specifically to sex work. 68% of the respondents reported that their only means of income prior to COVID-19 was sex work, putting them in a precarious situation given the fact that it is more difficult or impossible to receive unemployment if you do not have adequate proof of work. Additionally, 62% reported that sex work is still their only means of income even during the COVID-19 pandemic. This means that sex workers are having to resort to risking their own health and the health of their loved ones to remain financially stable due to the pandemic as opposed to being able to file for unemployment if sex work was considered a legitimate profession by the federal government.

We inquired about whether or not they had been receiving financial support from regular clients without seeing them in person. Although 43% responded no, 32% reported yes they received money as a gift, 17% reported their regular clients have been paying them for phone, text, or video services/content, and 8% reported that their regular clients have prepaid for future sessions.

We wanted to get a sense of what the clientele pool looked like during the pandemic so we asked what kind of client inquiries the respondents were still receiving. A majority (62%) reported that they were taking new clients that were trying to book with no regard for health risks, 44% said regular clients trying to book with no regard for health risks, 43% said regular clients trying to book who inquire or provide some information about the respondents or their health risks, 32% said clients who are lying or being coercive to try to get respondents to provide unsafe services, 23% were new clients who tried to book and provided or asked for some information about the respondents or their own virus risk, and only 19% responded that they had received no inquiries. This feedback is alarming as a wide breadth of the respondents reported they were receiving inquiries from clients who showed little or no regard for the health risks at hand. Sex workers are being put in tough situations where they have to either risk their own health and safety or pass on much-needed clients during a time with little to no work.

The two graphs depicted here show the change in types of sex work that respondents were participating in prior to and during the COVID-19 pandemic.   It is apparent that although many individuals continued to do in-person work, more people attempted to transition to more online-based work, such as phone sex operating, findomming/datadomming, or cam-modeling.

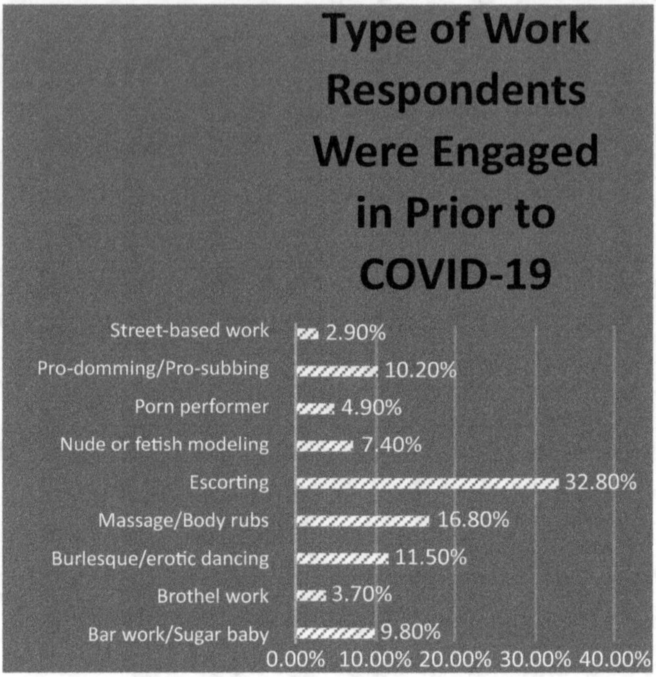
Type of Work Respondents Were Engaged in Prior to COVID-19
Street-based work
2.90%
Pro-domming/Pro-subbing
10.20%
Porn performer
4.90%
Nude or fetish modeling
7.40%
Escorting
32.80%
Massage/Body rubs
16.80%
Burlesque/erotic dancing
11.50%
Brothel work
3.70%
Bar work/Sugar baby
9.80%
0.00% 10.00% 20.00% 30.00% 40.00%

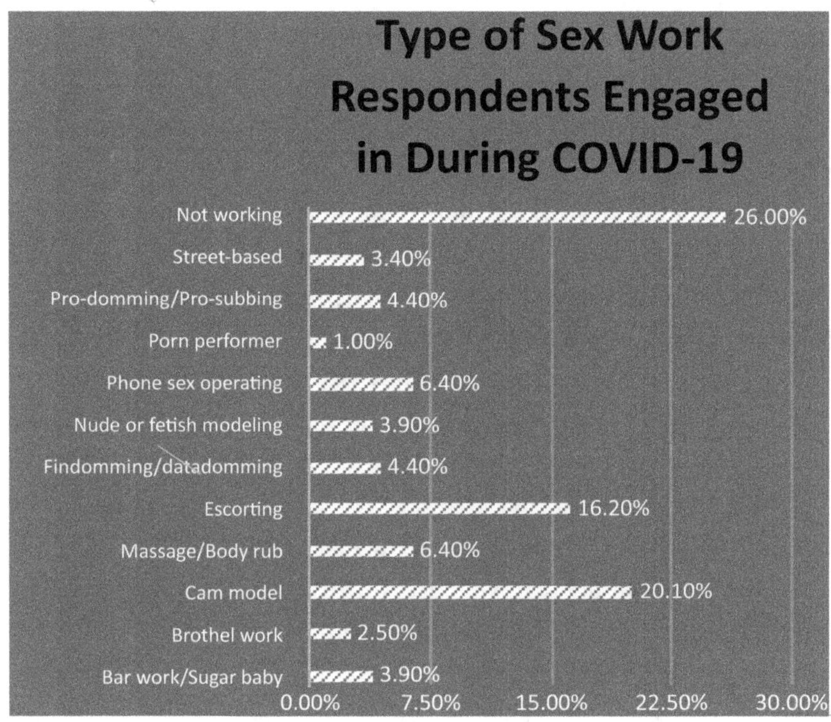

Mental Health During COVID-19

COVID-19 has exacerbated mental health issues around the globe, so we decided to inquire about respondents' level of distress during the pandemic. We asked them to rate their distress on a scale of 1-10, with 10 being the most distressed and 1 being the least. Most respondents' answers fell above 5. Seven was the most common response (25%) and 3 was the lowest (2%). From this it is apparent that most of the respondent's mental health is compromised during the pandemic, whether that be due to financial stress, fear of contracting the disease, distress from isolation, or other related mental health issues.

Domestic, Emotional, and Physical Abuse During COVID-19

Given the nature of social distancing, many people have been forced to remain in harmful situations at home where they receive physical or mental domestic abuse. 89% of respondents reported that they did not experience domestic violence, however, 3% have experienced the same domestic violence as before, 4% reported the domestic violence situation has been exacerbated by the pandemic, and 4% reported they experienced domestic violence in their relationship for the first time during the pandemic.

As for harm and violence received at the hand of clients, 28% reported they experienced new harm or violence after the onset of COVID-19. Some respondents elaborated on the harm they have been receiving from clients:

> *"Some of the clients want unsafe sex and if I say no they just fuck me anyway and dont pay me also I have to do ass work which is something I never did before."*

> *"Harassing by text and phone."*

> *'Now that you need money, will you finally do those things you said NO to before?'*

> *"They make me work for less money and a lot of them fuck me in the ass and is I refused they hit me real hard I got bruises to prove it, they know that I need the money and that I can't go to the police. Some don't pay me at all and I am afraid all the time of getting kill because a lot of the clients I don't know anything about."*

"I had a client rob me via a PayPal chargeback after the virus lockdown went to effect. It was 1700."

"I saw a regular client a few days ago for the first time since COVID-19 he started increasingly drinking until drunk, started screaming in my face, and physically pushed me out his front door."

Even for respondents who have not been taking clients, the client's negligence of sex workers' health is a serious concern, "I haven't seen any clients. But, I find it irritating that they keep contacting me to see when I am going to work again when we are all still at risk to spread Covid-19. And that they aren't really concerned about my safety and welfare."

Stigmatization of Sex Work During COVID-19

Similar to the HIV/AIDS epidemic, we were wondering if the COVID-19 pandemic had caused any increased stigmatization of sex work in society. 30% of respondents reported "yes" and were given the capacity to elaborate if they chose to do so:

"Some know what work I do and tell me to keep away from them because they think that I am sick"

"People making 'casual'' comments like 'I'm sure you're even more at risk.'"

"My partner demonizes me for even thinking about working at any point in the future. I can't even mention my work without him getting angry and accusing me of being a disease vector or worse. Millions of people are unemployed

and 10 years ago I started escorting because I was in debt and had no way out, and I improved my life so much and I was so stable. Now I am lost and financially decimated, and I can't even talk about it because I'm accused of being disgusting and dangerous. And when I see other sex workers on Facebook shaming people on the street for not wearing masks, I know damn well they won't be receptive to my desperation to start working again."

"Only from other SWers. One girl actually called someone a "disease vector" for working during the pandemic."

"People are saying we are spreading disease and saying 'just like we used to spread aids'."

Not only are sex workers receiving increased stigmatization from non-sex workers, but even sex workers themselves are demonizing and stigmatizing those that work during the pandemic, even if that is many people's only option to make ends meet.

Next, we asked about whether or not respondents are still taking clients, and if so what types of clients and what precautions are they taking to minimize risks of contracting COVID-19. 60% of the respondents reported that they are not still taking clients in person, only 2% reported that they are taking in-person clients because they believe the coronavirus is a conspiracy theory, 10% reported taking in-person clients because they are not high risk, and 29% reported taking in-person clients because they have no other options.

We then inquired about safety precautions respondents that are still having in-person clients are taking:

- 54% have clients wash their hands when they arrive

- 40% have clients shower when they arrive

- 14% have clients wear a face mask

- 16% wear a facemask themselves

- 51% have a no kissing rule

- 46% ask them about their recent travel and social distancing measures they are taking

- 32% only see a certain number of clients a day

- 40% disinfect incall between clients

- 13% outcall only

- 48% reported other measures or additional measures and elaborated:

"Dom only clients in person due to the convenience. No skin contact. Masks required at all times. Complete sterilization of all surfaces and items also placed in two UV germicidal cabinets in addition to usual cleaning and disinfection."

"I also purchased an infrared thermometer to take temps."

"I remain clothed, not mutual touch. in addition to the above things."

"Limiting the number of my sessions to two per week, to lower the probability."

Increased recruitment by pimps was another concern during such a financially insecure time, 18% of respondents answered "yes" when asked whether or not they have seen an increase in recruitment by pimps during the pandemic. Of those that responded "yes", only 9% reported they felt they were more vulnerable to their advances than before and 4% reported they have begun working with a pimp since after the shutdown. 21% of respondents also reported that they have been forced to take riskier clients since the onset of the pandemic. 9% reported that their regular clients are still calling at the same rate, 56% reported yes but not as much as usual, 26% said their phone doesn't ring at all anymore, and 8% said it was slow for a while but things are picking up again.

Given the mass transition to online work in other professional fields, we asked whether or not individuals had transitioned to online sex work: 7% responded yes and that they have been able to make ends meet, 17% responded yes, but that they have not been able to make ends meet from just doing online work, 16% have done a combination of online and in-person sex work, 45% said no, that they have relied on savings and/or aid, 15% responded no and that they have continued working in-person. Some chose to elaborate on their specific situations giving explanations such as: they do not have the correct technology and equipment to effectively transition to online work, some responded that they have attempted to switch, but have not been very successful, and one respondent reported, "It takes years to build online work to the income.   I'm currently making so little it's not as much of an option as people think."

Prior to COVID-19, 80% of respondents screened their clients, however, during the pandemic this number dropped to 63% with 8% reporting yes but not as often. Additionally, 46% reported that clients have been trying to get lower rates and pushing personal boundaries during the pandemic.   Some anecdotes from respondents include:

> *"Yes now, all they want is fuck me in the ass with no protection at the beginning of the pandemic I use to say no and for my troubles, I got rape a couple of times now I just take it because I need the money."*

> *"One guy offered me 20% of my regular rate."*

> *"I have a client who now wants to pay my 1hr rate I had 10yrs ago for a 90min appt. He is still working and has income and I feel he is taking advantage of the situation."*

> *"One client has tried to date me, acting like we could be in a relationship, telling me he has all this money to spend but no one to get physical affection from...etc guilt trips. He once started talking suicidal."*

The pandemic has placed a lot of sex workers in precarious situations where they are having to risk their own safety by not screening clients and dealing with pushy clients who are not respecting their personal boundaries.

Recommendations from Sex Workers

We wanted to get input from the respondents on what measures they thought could be adopted by the federal government to ensure all sex workers are covered by the relief aid offered in the Care Act. Respondents were given a list of choices and the capacity to check all that apply: 85% of respondents noted they felt universal basic income for all adults would be helpful, 75% felt a rent freeze would be helpful, 65% reported eviction freezes would also be helpful, 67% reported coverage of COVID-19 related medical costs, 66% reported coverage of all medical costs, and 20% gave other suggestions. These other suggestions included Medicaid for all, student and consumer debt discharge, expanded housing assistance, legal assistance, expansion of unemployment benefits to cover non-traditional jobs (such as cleaning houses, childcare, or under-the-table jobs), and the suspension of the criminalization of sex work.

We also asked for their input on other policies they feel would benefit sex workers during the pandemic. It is important for legislators to know how sex workers are being affected by the COVID-19 pandemic and how the federal government can better provide services for sex workers during national crises, so we felt inquiring directly about this was a vital aspect of amplifying the voices of sex workers during a global pandemic. Some of the suggestions they had include:

- Decriminalize sex work in general, but especially during such national crises.

- Treat sex work the same as any other profession and provide them with the same rights.

- Dismantle FOSTA

- Universal Basic Income

- Find ways to aid those with illegal immigration statuses and abolish ICE

- More community support surrounding mental health, emergency housing, emotional support, money management/planning in the environment of a pandemic, etc.

- Release of incarcerated individuals on prostitution-related charges

- Use abandoned hotels and buildings for the vulnerable homeless population

- End policing of sex work

- Free, accessible COVID-19 testing for everyone

The decriminalization and decarceration of sex work and those incarcerated due to sex work is something that needs to be addressed beyond the confines of the COVID-19 pandemic, however, during such a national crisis, it is more important than ever that sex workers are able to receive unemployment and be treated as real professionals with jobs covered by federal aid. Universal Basic Income, the abolition of ICE, mutual/community aid, and accessible COVID-19 testing, are measures that would go beyond the scope of sex workers and benefit other marginalized groups as well. The needs of those involved in the sex industry thus overlap and are intertwined with other issues facing our society on the whole and should be addressed now more than ever as the entire globe is suffering through one of the largest global crises in history.

Conclusion

The COVID-19 pandemic has exacerbated the challenges that vulnerable populations face. Although COVID-19 has affected everyone, there are certain groups that have been impacted more than others. Sex workers fall under the category of vulnerable populations that have been impacted immensely by COVID-19 and that have oftentimes fallen through the cracks in terms of receiving adequate aid from the federal government during such a precarious time. In order to amplify the voices of sex workers and learn directly from those most impacted about what exact measures can and should be taken by the government during these difficult times, we issued out the survey that we have analyzed in this chapter to help better understand how the coronavirus has affected the sex industry.

The criminalization of sex work, stigmatization, and belief that sex work is not real work that prevails in this country has prevented many sex workers from receiving adequate assistance during the pandemic, forcing many sex workers to take on clients and put themselves in harm's way just to make ends meet.

Chapter 13: Policy Recommendations

"Sex workers need to be listened to and respected, our jobs do not impair our ability to know ourselves and we are not in need of rescue, simply more options."

Survey Participant

Policy Recommendations for Lawmakers

Decriminalize All Consensual Adult Prostitution, Including Third Parties

The obvious solution is to decriminalize sex workers, their decriminalization, a sex worker who was assaulted could report it to the police without fear that her driver or roommate or partner or child would be arrested for "trafficking" her, a client who encountered a trafficking victim could report it to the police without fear of being arrested and made an example of, and a driver who encountered a trafficking victim or witnessed an assault clients, their families, their working together, their drivers, their security, and their bookers and screeners. Under could also report it to the police or offer testimony as a witness without fearing being charged with "trafficking" themselves, their colleagues or fellow victims, or being forced to register as sex offenders.

The complete decriminalization of all consenting adult prostitution is recommended by Amnesty International (their research on the topic is available on their website), the American Civil Liberties Union, the Human Rights Campaign, UNAIDS, UN Working Group on Discrimination Against Women and Girls, and the World Health Organization. Countries that have decriminalized consenting adult sex work, like New Zealand, have seen a huge reduction in or complete elimination of sex trafficking and sex workers there are able to access the equal protection of labor laws.

Harm Reduction: Immunity in Reporting Crimes

Where prostitution can't be decriminalized yet, a harm reduction measure is to allow sex workers, sex trafficking victims, their clients, and associates to report crimes like sex trafficking, murder, sexual assault, and child pornography without being arrested for prostitution. Currently many sex workers report that they have been the victim or witness of a crime they haven't reported out of fear of police. Their fears aren't unfounded - of sex workers who have reported crimes, a large percent report being turned away, threatened with arrest, and some report being arrested while trying to report that they had been the victim or witness of a crime. These injustices happen to sex trafficking survivors at a higher rate than other sex workers.

If the criminal justice community believes that sex workers are all victims in need of rescue, they must allow sex workers to report crimes without arresting the sex worker, her colleagues, clients, employees, or family. Sex workers are important partners in working towards public safety, and their reports need to be taken seriously.

Similarly, clients' reports should be taken seriously and without threat of arrest or public shaming. Victims of the most horrific kinds of sex trafficking are typically very isolated, with little to no access to phones. The only people they are ever alone with are often clients, and it may take several visits before a victim trusts a client enough to confide in him. Currently the zeitgeist leans towards that client being publicly shamed and charged with a felony if he calls police. Lawmakers should understand that any efforts to alienate clients from law enforcement are efforts to prevent the reporting of sex trafficking and ultimately increase sex trafficking.

Harm Reduction: Removing Barriers to Exiting the Sex Industry

If all you know about sex trafficking and "rescue" is what you see on television, you wouldn't think that it is easier to get away from a pimp and have a good life than it is to get away from a prostitution charge and have a good life. Unfortunately, that is the lived reality of many sex workers and sex trafficking survivors. A prostitution charge follows you and its stigma and resulting discrimination can make it almost impossible to obtain housing, employment, and even child custody. Although prostitution is a low level misdemeanor in almost every jurisdiction, it's often referred to as a life sentence because it leaves the sex workers and sex trafficking survivors charged with it disenfranchised from equal protection under the law and restricts social and economic mobility, leaving them trapped in underground economies.

To clear the path for the most marginalized of sex workers and sex trafficking survivors to leave the industry, it's essential that every state create a mechanism to remove prostitution charges from the public record in a timely and accessible manner.

Enhanced Sentencing for Perpetrators

"I picked prostitutes as victims because they were easy to pick up, without being noticed," the Green River Killer said during his confession. "I knew they would not be reported missing right away, and might never be reported missing." Encouraging victims and witnesses to report crimes against sex workers and sex trafficking victims is only the beginning. Once crimes are reported, they must be thoroughly investigated and the perpetrator must be charged. To accomplish this, crimes against sex workers and sex trafficking survivors should be viewed as hate crimes and there should be enhanced criminal penalties for those who target us.

Currently, even when investigators do a perfect investigation and bring it to prosecutors, perpetrators often are not charged, or are allowed ridiculous plea deals. This is because prosecutors believe that juries do not find sex workers or sex trafficking victims to be relatable victims. Judges, juries, and prosecutors have often expressed that crimes against people in sex work are lesser crimes or non-crimes. This long history of very reduced or no criminal penalties for violent crimes against sex workers and sex trafficking victims must be corrected by instructing police, prosecutors, and juries, that crimes against people in sex work are more serious and should have greater penalties.

Understanding Safety Models vs Trafficking

Many things that sex workers do for safety are now criminalized as trafficking or as felony promoting prostitution or pandering under many state laws. In some cases, independent adult sex workers have been charged with felony promoting prostitution or sex trafficking of themselves for things like aiding or facilitating their own prostitution, advertising their own prostitution, or having a place of their own prostitution. This causes workers to take less safety measures and prevents them from reporting serious crimes when they are victims or witnesses.

Imagine that you and a friend were sharing a hotel room for work, and she got a call from a customer seeking a duo. You agree and during the appointment, the client shows both of you child pornography on his phone. Afterwards your friend wants to call the police, but you remind her that you're both working in her hotel room (having a place of prostitution is felony promoting prostitution, pandering, or sex trafficking in most jurisdictions) and that she booked the call for both of you (obtaining a prostitute for a client is felony promoting prostitution or sex trafficking in most jurisdictions). Do you think your friend still wants to call the police and risk being charged with two felonies and becoming a registered sex offender?

Things like kidnapping, sexual assault, and labor trafficking are already criminalized. Sex trafficking victims don't need special laws criminalizing everyone around them. They simply need to be treated like any other victim when they are kidnapped, assaulted, extorted, threatened, labor trafficked, etc. Creating an aggravator or sentence enhancer ("hate crime legislation") when victims are targeted because they are in sex work can achieve this.

What Not to Do: The Nordic Model/End Demand

The Nordic Model, also called the Swedish Model and End Demand, sounds simple at first: just arrest the customers. Now imagine if an anti-trafficking group proposed eliminating trafficking in the carnival industry (where it is higher than in the sex industry) by arresting people who go to carnivals. Would that make sense?

Clients of sex workers are our first responders. They should be incentivized to report sex trafficking to the police, not arrested for it. Policy that alienates sex workers, sex trafficking victims, and their clients from accessing the equal protections of criminal justice law is policy that increases sex trafficking.

In 2016 Amnesty International released a report of its research in Norway. It found that the End Demand model resulted in several human rights violations. Under End Demand sex workers were subject to increased violence, evictions, exploitation, stigma, discrimination, and police harassment and control. Sex worker's normal safety precautions became impossible to carry out. Good customers became rare and violent criminals posing as customers increased. As a trafficking response, Amnesty International found that the Nordic Model is ineffective: it decreases reporting to police, increases sex workers' vulnerability to traffickers, and deports victims with no regard to prosecuting their traffickers.

Sex Trafficking of Minors: Understanding Misleading Information

Under the Violence Against Women Act, youth who exchange sex for things like housing, food, clothing, or drugs are defined as sex trafficking victims, even though there is usually no criminal trafficking statute to charge anyone with in these situations. Minors who work in the sex industry on their own or with peers are also defined as sex trafficking victims under VAWA. When you see studies quoting huge numbers of child sex trafficking victims, dig into the research methodology and you will find that the definition of sex trafficking that they are using is a variant of this federal definition and does not align with criminal or popular definitions of sex trafficking. Using misleading definitions to conflate most runaway youth with the abuse of children in the sex industry can help agencies get funding, but it does not help the youth in question.

These youth fall into distinct groups:

- Those who've traded sex for survival - for example, a 17-year-old who runs away from foster care and has sex with a 19-year-old boyfriend so that she can live with him.

- Those who've had others trade sexual access to them - for example a parent, guardian, or friend who trades sexual access to the minor for housing or drugs.

- Those who have engaged in the sex industry on their own or working with peers - for example, a 17-year-old who runs away from a group home and engages in prostitution with her friends to survive.

- Those who have been forced, coerced, or tricked into the commercial sex industry or who have been abused within the industry or had another person profit from their prostitution.

These groups have very different needs. When they are lumped together and branded as sex trafficking victims, the policy response can be harmful to the large majority who are engaging in survival sex rather than being forced into prostitution. Research in urban centers has found that only 10% of minor sex trafficking victims have engaged in prostitution, and only 10% of them (or 1% of the whole) work with adult third parties, and only 1% of them (or one tenth of one percent of the whole) identify as having been forced or pressured into prostitution.

Anyone interested in this topic should read *Domestic Minor Sex Trafficking: Beyond Victims and Villains*, by Dr. Alix Lutnick.

Trafficking Prevention: Housing, Services, Equality

Adults and youth become vulnerable to trafficking or other abuses in the sex industry in the same ways that people become vulnerable to any other kind of abuse: they have been cast out and pushed to the edge of the herd. They are easy picking for predators. A very large percentage of minor sex trafficking survivors are LGBTQ. In *Surviving The Streets of New York*, researchers found that the primary event that led to the LGBTQ youth they studied trading sex was being kicked out of or discriminated against by a shelter.

Women being released from jail without community support or housing are at risk, as are others experiencing homelessness and food insecurity, disability, a criminal record, or another marginalized identity. A poor economy or having a family to support can mean that someone who would rather not do sex work sees it as their only viable option. Community resilience work is anti-trafficking work.

Policy for Police and Prosecutors

Sexual Misconduct by Police Officers

Sexual conduct by those making prostitution arrests should be criminalized as sexual assault and prosecuted as such. There must be clear and safe ways for sex workers and sex trafficking survivors to report sexual misconduct or coercion by police officers to a regulatory agency outside of the police department. Repeatedly activists have seen predators in uniform work themselves into positions of authority as "saviors" of children, sex trafficking survivors, and sex workers. Survivors fear that if they try to report they will not be believed or will be retaliated against, and departments can rarely be trusted to investigate themselves.

COUNT 1: PRACTICING/ASSIGNATION
To Wit: ▓▓▓▓▓▓▓ did knowingly engage in prostitution or assignation, which is in violation of Anchorage Municipal Code 8.65.020.A.
    This complaint is based on witness information provided by Det. R. Dojaque and/or this complaint is based on personal observations of the complaining witness. The defendant engaged in assignation by doing oral sex and vaginal sex for $100.00.

An example of a prostitution sting that should have criminal penalties for the officers involved.

Sexual conduct during prostitution stings has been found to be a violation of due process in state courts. It is particularly reprehensible when police claim to be doing prostitution stings to "rescue" sex trafficked minors. Officers who engage in this sort of behavior are morally unfit to be entrusted with public safety.

Encouraging Reports from Sex Workers

Even in states that don't have immunity in reporting laws, police and prosecutors can issue joint statements that sex workers, sex trafficking survivors, and our colleagues will not be arrested or prosecuted when making reports of serious crimes against people. Police literally mislead us as part of their jobs, so a public statement reassures us that they will follow through and can be held accountable for such in the media. This kind of action is especially important when a serial killer or rapist is targeting sex workers, or if addressing sex trafficking is a priority.

Policy for Shelters and Social Services

Don't Work with Police

When shelters and social service agencies work with police, they lose the trust of sex workers and sex trafficking survivors who feel "hunted" by police or who have been victimized by police. When these providers start calling the police on their clients for being sex trafficking victims, it can result in the arrest of victims.

Don't Discriminate

When critical services are denied to sex workers it can place them immediately into a situation where they may have to engage in riskier or unwanted sex work.

Don't Assume

Don't assume that we are either victims or empowered superheroes. Some of us hate our jobs and don't identify as victims, while others may love our jobs and still identify as victims. Many people who have been sex trafficked also find sex work to be a good career. We are all allowed to have days where we hate our jobs, just like everyone else, without having our whole existence called into question.

Unaccompanied Minors

Many shelters have a policy that youth cannot stay if they don't provide their guardian's contact information. For those rare youth who are actually forced into prostitution, it is usually by a parent or guardian. These youth are often excluded from shelter services because they won't provide their traffickers' contact information.

Supporting Resilience

Don't curse your clients by trying to convince them they are powerless pathetic victims. Instead, support resilience.

Suggested Reading

We have created a suggested reading list for you at:

https://coyoteri.org/suggested-reading/

About COYOTE RI

Call Off Your Old Tired Ethics, Rhode Island (COYOTE RI) is a group of current and former sex workers, sex trafficking survivors, and our allies advocating for policies that promote the health and safety of people involved in the sex industry.

Follow us on social media:

https://coyoteri.substack.com/
https://www.threads.net/@coyote_ri
https://x.com/Coyoteri
https://www.instagram.com/coyote_ri/?hl=en
https://www.facebook.com/coyoteri

Podcast
https://open.spotify.com/show/03P2FVG5OoyVWRJ23ZKVvy

Afterword

by Tatiana Rothchild

Exemplifying Community-Led Research

Research on systematically excluded communities, whether conducted by academics or policymakers, all too often ignores the priorities, preferences, or realities of the community it examines. "Re-search" so often situates people "as specimens, rather than people.[8]" Especially in the case of criminalized, stigmatized, or otherwise marginalized groups, conventional approaches to research reinforce the uneven power dynamics that led to the project and can, at its worst, do harm to the communities it "re-searches."

Academics have used "community-placed research," "community-based research," and "participatory research" to describe projects moving away from the harmful, specimen centered elements of traditional research approaches.[9] Participatory research moves beyond simply being placed or based in the communities it claims to study, but members of the community in question are active in the design and implementation of the project.

 "Community-led research" (CLR) like this prioritizes the expertise and lived experiences of members of the community in question,

---

[8] "Decolonising research methodology must include undoing its dirty history." https://theconversation.com/decolonising-research-methodology-must-include-undoing-its-dirty-history-83912.

[9] "Community-Based Research Continuum" University of Iowa Human Subjects Office. Accessed 4 March 2024. https://hso.research.uiowa.edu/community-based-research-continuum.

which results in more accurate and relevant findings and mitigates harm that research can inflict.

This book represents an edited collection of CLR projects, hosted by a sex worker led organization, organized by sex worker academics trained in social science research, focused on creating pathways for sex workers and trafficking survivors to tell their own stories in their own words. This approach inherently centers the voices of community members and challenges dominant processes and narratives on what is important to know and ask. CLR projects like this book streamline problems that academics face in reaching communities and building trust to conduct authentic research; resulting in findings that externally located researchers may not have access to; and challenging existing societal and institutional power dynamics as communities build the research questions and processes. In these ways, CLR pursues stronger research than academia alone can create, and challenges the echo chamber of elite "discovery[10]" that academic publications encourage research to become. CLR answers questions that academics may not consider or prioritize and mitigates harmful practices by challenging, rather than reinforcing, uneven power structures.

Sex workers have engaged in their own research and information sharing for a long time. Like many systemically excluded communities, the goals of such communication have included maximizing their own protection, strategizing their business management, and coordinating on policy making. This book serves as an excellent example of a well-designed, comprehensive project

---

[10] "'The literature' is a construct, and finding a gap in it means discovering that a group of relatively powerful people doesn't know something, as opposed to discovering something that is a universal unknown." - Anna Meier @AnnaMeierPS, 20 March 2023 on Twitter.

that prioritizes the questions around safety, stigma, access, and policy that sex workers and sex worker rights organizations have chosen to prioritize. It includes the widest and most comprehensive, largest survey of sex workers in the U.S. up to this point, and compares and triangulates those findings with regionally specific surveys. The research process, findings, and policy recommendations presented in this work push back on exclusionary practices and policies and illustrate how important community driven research should be to academics and policymakers.

Prioritizing Self-Identification and Important Group Distinctions

The presentation of research participants and subsequent findings in this book illustrate an important distinguishing trend that the research team at COYOTE RI has been implementing in their projects for years. While many academics and policymakers have lumped together different groups under legal and research definitions, the projects represented here distinguish between groups to highlight different experiences, different needs, and different findings among different groups. The distinctions reviewed include the type of sex work a participant engaged in; disaggregated demographic data to show differences in age, gender, race, and other elements; and perhaps most principally, a distinction between people who have undergone force, fraud, or coercion within the sex industry and those who have not, including those who entered the industry as minors.

This latter shift pushes back against many state and non-criminal legal definition of sex trafficking and against sex-worker exclusionary religious and feminist movements in nonprofit spaces that attempt to negate or reduce sex worker agency in the anti-human trafficking field. The federal legal definition of sex trafficking includes any minor who has survival sex, whether or not there is prostitution, force, fraud, or coercion present, creating a non-criminal definition of sex trafficking - a point that many sex workers have pushed back on. This definition obscures the structural and institutional factors that bring minors to the sex industry and makes sex workers who attempt to help minors in the sex industry even more targeted by institutions. Additionally, some service providers inflate the number of sex trafficking victims they serve by mis-identifying sex workers as sex trafficking victims (a point many of the research participants shared experiences around). The distinctions between these groups are foundational as sex workers describe their own experiences, but are revolutionary in academic and policy spaces, where sex workers voices, criticisms, and recommendations have been ignored and sidelined for so long. COYOTE research stands out among other ongoing research endeavors as they repeat these distinguished group dynamics in different research projects they oversee.

Bringing National Trends to Light

This book tells a story of community-led research that began at the local and state levels and grew to review national trends in sex workers' experiences. Chapters 1 and 2 describe the start of this research in Alaska and Rhode Island, sharing findings from the more localized projects that laid the foundation for the national survey. Chapters 3 and 4 share findings on the demographics and social dynamics of the participants of the national survey. Chapters 5 and 6 focus on the experiences of sex worker participants in different areas of work, victimization, and criminalization. Chapters 7 - 9 describe the legal structures that sex workers live and work under and their experiences under certain changing laws, particularly FOSTA. Chapters 10 and 11 outline research on institutional services provided under the guise of assisting sex workers, and evaluate whether this aligns with actual experiences by participants. Chapter 12 reviews the disproportionate impact of COVID-19 on sex workers. Importantly for policymakers, the book ends in Chapter 13 with a summary of the policy recommendations with which each topical area of research concludes, bringing together overall suggestions that sex workers communities nationally are pushing for.

This book represents different research projects and foci implemented through community led processes and brought together to share a narrative told by sex workers about sex workers. It pushes back on harmful and exploitative practices in the anti-human trafficking community; makes strong policy recommendations around sex work and sex trafficking backed by evidence from sex workers and trafficking survivors themselves; and illustrates the ways that community research should be done, not just including community members as token advisors to give feedback on design and implementation, but following research questions put forth by the community itself and led by community researchers who drive the project fully. This book holds lessons for academics on strong research processes and lessons for elected policymakers on how best to serve the sex workers and sex trafficking survivors they represent.

Authors and Editors

Bella Robinson is a sex worker, sex trafficking survivor, and the Executive Director of the Rhode Island Chapter of Call Off Your Old Tired Ethics (COYOTE-RI). She founded COYOTE RI in 2009 in response to Rhode Island re-criminalizing prostitution. Bella is a previously incarcerated person who was a victim of state-sponsored violence. Her personal experiences with the criminal justice system over the past four decades give her exceptional expertise in the areas of sex worker rights organizing.

Tara Burns, MA is an Alaskan sex worker, sex trafficking survivor, and researcher. She was the first registered lobbyist in the state of Alaska to lobby for the rights of sex workers. She has been COYOTE RI's research and policy director since 2020.

Tatiana Rothchild is a PhD candidate in Political Science at Northeastern University. Her research focuses on human trafficking at national and international levels, particularly in areas of problem framing, state coercion, workers' rights, human rights audit culture, and international policy models. She is passionate about challenging state violence, particularly in areas where institutions claim moral credibility and reputational gains for participating in violence.

Meghan Peterson, MPH is a public health researcher and a sex worker rights advocate and graduate of Brown University School of Public Health, class of 2018.   Previously, she worked on campaigns related to healthcare access at the AIDS Foundation of Chicago and SWOP-Chicago. She researches the effects of incarceration on public health, particularly surrounding overdose mortality and HIV outcomes. Her graduate thesis work focused on perceptions of drug-induced homicide laws among people who use drugs and who are incarcerated

A. Horning, Ph.D., is an Assistant Professor of Criminology and Justice Studies at the University of Massachusetts Lowell. For the last decade, they have researched risk as it pertains to hidden populations, such as social actors in commercial sex markets, unaccompanied minor refugees, and migrants. They have been published in journals such as *Trends in Organized Crime, Critical Criminology*, and *Deviant Behavior*. Dr. Horning is the Principal Investigator of a large-scale funded project about commercial sex markets in New York City and Chicago and projects exploring the European and US "refugee crises." They explore the intersections of social science research methods and visual arts in public sociology projects, including *Precarious Record and Civil Society*. Dr. Ruf's unique background and ability to conduct qualitative and quantitative studies enable them to engage in high-level interdisciplinary research utilizing innovative mixed methods approaches.

Placidina Fico graduated from UMass Boston in Women & Gender Studies in 2015 and completed her Master in Public Health at Boston University in 2019. Passionate about sexual and reproductive justice, she volunteered with the Eastern Massachusetts Abortion Fund as a case manager (2017-2019) and the Boston Abortion Support Collective as an abortion doula (2017-2021). She currently serves as a Community Advisory Board member for Partners in Contraceptive Choice in Knowledge, a state initiative to improve contraceptive access and equity in Massachusetts, and as a helpline volunteer for the Abortion Support Network in Europe. Placidina has extensive research experience in sexual and reproductive health and rights, HIV prevention, and public health interventions.

Madison Hough (she/her) is currently pursuing her MA in Fashion Curation and Cultural Programming at the London College of Fashion after receiving her A.B. in Anthropology and International & Public Affairs from Brown University in 2022. Madison is committed to pushing boundaries in fashion curation, where her interests lie at the nexus of gender and sexuality studies, decolonising the museum, and the anthropology of dress.

Allie Benz (she/they) received her MA in International Human Rights. She is currently working as a data analyst at the Denver Public Library. Her interests lie in the intersection of quantitative data and DEI work, primarily in the context of gender and sexuality.

Kayli Wren (they/them) found COYOTE and got involved while living in Providence and studying at Brown University. They currently live in Philadelphia and work for a health tech company that provides care coordination for queer and trans healthcare needs.

Chloe Kim (she/her) is a junior at Brown University studying Public Health. She is primarily interested in addressing health disparities to provide better health outcomes for systemically underrepresented and underserved populations, and her research interests include the intersection between disability justice, biomedical informatics, and sexual/reproductive health! In her free time, she likes to make music, eat new foods, and explore Providence!